Turn Left at
the Devil Tree

Turn Left at the Devil Tree

Derek Pugh

With a foreword by
Ted Egan AO

National Library of Australia Cataloguing-in-Publication entry

Author: Pugh, Derek, author

Title: Turn left at the devil tree : a memoir / Derek Pugh ; Ted Egan AO.

ISBN: 9780992355807

Subjects: Pugh, Derek.
Teachers--Northern Territory--Arnhem Land--Biography.
Teaching--Northern Territory--Arnhem Land.
Arnhem Land (N.T.)--Education.
Arnhem Land (N.T.)--Social life and customs.
Arnhem Land (N.T.)--Social conditions.
Arnhem Land (N.T.)--History.

Other Authors/Contributors:
Egan, Ted, 1932-

Dewey Number: 371.10092

Also by Derek Pugh
Tammy Damulkurra, 1995 (2nd edition 2013)
The Owner's Guide to the Teenage Brain, 2011

Contact

derekpugh1@gmail.com

Website

www.derekpugh.com.au

ACKNOWLEDGMENTS

My thanks go to those who freely offered help, advice and support throughout the writing process, particularly to: Liz Pugh, Mark Heyward, Mervin Gilham and my late father Roy Pugh who were early critical readers of the text; Pierro Serra, a fine editor; Dr Murray Garde, for his advice on Kunwinjku language and his help as a colleague back in the day; Ted Egan, who was in Maningrida at the beginning, for his pre-dawn phone conversations, his foreword and his invaluable suggestions and the correction of a fact or two.

Thanks also to the stars of this book, the Kunwinjku and Burarra peoples who were so hospitable and patient in my clumsy attempts to join in with Arnhem Land Life.

CONTENT WARNING
Australian Indigenous people are warned that some individuals who are now deceased are named in this book. I have used real names in all but one case (either with permission or because their names are in the public domain) because I believe their descendents will want to know about them.

CONTENTS

FOREWORD

Derek Pugh has written an admirable book on two counts. It is a rattling good yarn and at the same time it is a fine teacher's handbook. From the moment he takes the momentous decision to accept a teaching posting at Maningrida, in remote central Arnhem Land, Australia. Derek develops the best possible tactics in such situations. Don't throw your weight around too much; learn from the locals; don't have too big an opinion of yourself; be a good listener and, as Monty Python would tell us, "Always Look on the Bright Side of Life."

I have a great affection for Maningrida. I went there myself, in 1957, for a mere six months, as a patrol officer in the party that established the remote outpost. Darwin – three days west, by boat only, in those days – is the capital of the Northern Territory. At the time many of the 'bush' First Australians from the Maningrida region had left their traditional country and were living on the fringes of the city, getting into lots of mischief, as 'fringe dwellers' do. It was decided that a 'station' be started in their own country, on the Liverpool River, a place where they could retain their traditional links with the land, but have access to the basic things from the western world that they had come to covet – tobacco, western foodstuffs, clothing. At the same time they would be free from that scourge of Aboriginal society, alcohol.

We took a few 'local' Aboriginals 'back to country' on a little lugger named *Temora* and they helped us set up a primitive camp at a traditional well named Maningrida, on the banks of the Liverpool River. One of the locals was a young boy who subsequently became known as "Doctor Jimmy" – he features in Derek's book – for he helped Ingrid Drysdale, a magnificent member of our small foundation party, as she undertook the task of treating the sick, particularly those unfortunates who had contracted leprosy. Ingrid and Doctor Jimmy were a magnificent team.

My job was to find out just how many people there were in the region – within 200 miles in any given direction – and record where they were living. It's not so long ago, but many Aboriginals in the region wore no clothing at all. They were still totally capable of living off the land – and the sea – for this is the home of mud crabs, oysters, barramundi and other succulent fish. And they lived well. Food and water were easily available to such skilled hunters and gatherers. Crocodiles were the principal hazard, but the people understood and respected these survivors from the dinosaur age.

We had been there only a few days when Doctor Jimmy ran up to me with his eyes bulging. "Naked blackfellows!" he shouted, as he pointed along the beach. There were five men, cleverly standing in the open so we could see them, but out of spear range. Indeed, they were stark naked. I asked one of the older men to go and greet our first visitors and offer them hospitality: I wanted to talk to them and perhaps visit them in their own country. They came in and we shook hands. We offered them a cup of tea and they accepted. Ingrid Drysdale, a godly woman, was a bit embarrassed. She went to her tent and came back with a roll of red turkey twill material. She cut off a square meter of material for each man and handed it to him, obviously thinking they would wrap it around their nether regions, as good 'mission' blackfellows would understand. Solemnly, they accepted the material and each one converted the red cloth into a prestigious headband.

Maningrida was still about as primitive as that when Derek arrived. Fortunately, he fitted in well with the local people immediately, aware that he was a participant in an immense cultural experience, introducing stone-age people to western habits. At the same time he was able to observe at close quarters the incredible affiliation with their environment they had developed over thousands of years' of knowledge and ceremony.

It was frustrating at times, but always a challenge, always fascinating and Derek has recorded his experiences beautifully in this delightful book. I am confident that it will sell well and be positively reviewed, but I entertain the hope that it is taken up seriously by education departments and used as a part of teacher training.

Teachers such as Derek are rare. Many people reminisce about particular teachers from their school days and approbation is usually driven by the knowledge that he or she, "... understood me: school was fun." I reckon there are many Aboriginal people in western Arnhem Land who would recall Derek Pugh with great affection on those grounds.

I recommend this book to readers of all ages, everywhere.

TED EGAN AO
ALICE SPRINGS

1

GOING BUSH

A rnhem Land is a large area of Australia's Northern Territory, vibrant with scattered communities and their outstations, containing descendents of Australia's first peoples – members of a dozen or more tribal groups with languages as distinct as the boundaries of their traditional tribal lands. Huge rivers flow from a rugged sandstone interior to the coast, draining forests and swamps and floodplains that so groan with bush foods they have made the local people resource rich for millennia. Nestled at the mouth of one of these rivers, the Liverpool, is a community of about 1500 people named Maningrida.

Maningrida is the major community in central Arnhem Land. It services an area of thousands of square kilometers, stretching south to the Stone Country, east to the Blyth River and west to the flood plains of the Liverpool and its confluence of the Mann River. In this enormous and largely unpopulated country, about thirty smaller communities - known

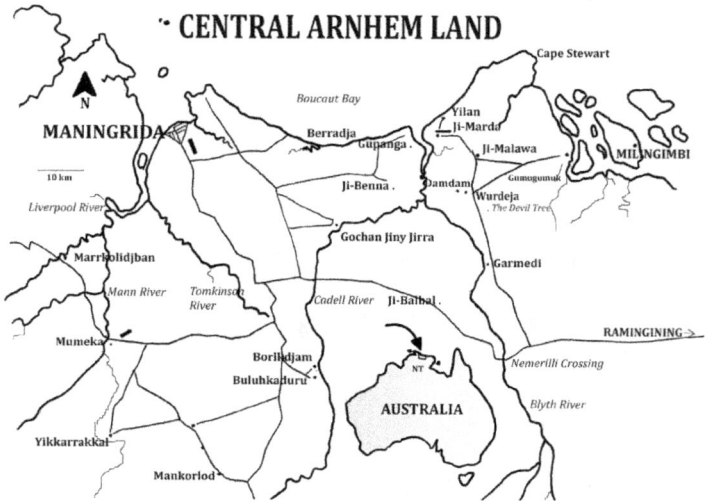

Central Arnhem Land Map

as outstations in my time but more commonly called *homeland centers* these days - have become permanent settlements for families jaded by town life or intent on maintaining as traditional a life as possible in the modern world.

As a young teacher in 1989, it was to go to this part of the world that I found myself packing my bags. I was seeking adventure and I was not to be disappointed. This book is the story of the life we lived there in the 1990s.

My non-Aboriginal colleagues and I were modern day people who arrived by plane. We watched television, used laptop computers with tiny black and white screens and eventually even called folks on our newly installed long distance telephones. But we looked back, in some cases as little as 40 years, into a time before European contact with some of the tribes of Arnhem Land and wondered at the adventures and experiences of others in an age that will never return. I wasn't a pioneer of the Northern Territory or Arnhem Land, but my hope is that in these pages I can record a sliver of time in one corner of the Territory that came and went relatively unmarked simply because we weren't the first or the extraordinary bush folk of the early years. Our experiences in the 1990s were events in everyday life and as the Territory has moved on, writing them adds to the never-ending tale that is history.

I lived for over ten years in Arnhem Land, more than half of them in Maningrida, working as a teacher in classrooms and in outstation schools and later as a Principal. Arnhem Land was proclaimed an Aboriginal Reserve in 1931 but was named by Matthew Flinders much earlier, after a Dutch ship, captained by William van Coolstcerat, had been blown off course to this coast in 1623. He could have called it *van Coolstcerat Land*, but Arnhem is easier to spell.

I first went to Arnhem Land in 1982. Fresh from a university graduation ceremony in Armidale, NSW, I had driven my Mini Moke across Australia and arrived in Jabiru just about in the height of the wet season. Jabiru is a uranium mining town in the middle of Kakadu National Park, ironically a world heritage area. The town was still under construction when I arrived and people lived close to the mine in Jabiru East, a temporary town of demountable buildings called *dongas*. I had a friend there from uni days and through her introduction I scored a job with the Land Conservation Unit of the Conservation Commission the day after I arrived. I was given my own donga in Kookaburra Street, and worked as a lab technician measuring erosion levels in a number of creek systems as part of base-data collection regarding the effects of mining in the region.

This led to other temporary work with the Office of the Supervising Scientist and a job as a ranger in Kakadu National Park based at the East Alligator Ranger Station. They were great short term jobs and one of the best parts of being a ranger was working with the kids who visited the park. School groups were always fun and wide-eyed with wonder and when they inspired me to return to college and get a teaching qualification I disappeared to Perth for a year. I returned to the Territory in 1985 and spent a few years in Alice Springs and Katherine, so didn't get back to Arnhem Land until my appointment at the Maningrida Community Education Center in July 1989.

Going back came as the result of an epiphany. I was teaching high school science and the matriculation biology class in Katherine High School. Katherine was a good place to live, but one day whilst I was teaching cyclic-photophosphorilation to a bunch of teenagers I made a decision. If your lips moved when you read that last sentence you'll understand my predicament. The bored expressions of those teenagers told me clearly that they thought there was more to life than the cyclic-photophosphorilation that allows it. It hit me then that they were right.

I'd only been back in Australia six months, after a year travelling through Asia and South America, and I was restless. I had long had an interest in looking for work in a different cultural context, and had already had the introductory interview with the Australian Volunteers Abroad organization, seeking something interesting in New Guinea, or the Maldives or somewhere. But then I thought, "Why not teach in third world Australia?"

That afternoon I applied for a transfer, but not to just anywhere. I wanted a small single-teacher school in a *dry* Aboriginal community. *Dry* referred to a community where the elders had banned the drinking of alcohol. In some communities this worked well; in others it meant a growing pile of green cans around the base of the 'No Grog' sign on the road outside of town so that the community still had to put up with the drunks, just not while they were drinking. Where *dry* meant no alcohol, I thought life would be peaceful, traditional and full of new experiences, with kids who would be as keen as mustard to learn and crying out for a fun school program. I pictured remote cattle station communities, a class of ten bright eyed children and all the hunting and fishing that I'd ever want.

I was green - a high school science teacher without any rural experience asking to go *really* bush and teach primary kids. The servants of the Department of Education weren't all fools. A few days later someone rang me.

"There's no school available like that for you, but how about an outstation job in Maningrida?"

"What's that?" I asked. I knew nothing about Maningrida except that it was in Arnhem Land. The only excursion I had made into Arnhem Land proper before was to Gunbalanya, just north of Kakadu when I was a ranger living at the East Alligator Ranger Station. That trip was to buy buffalo sausages at their butcher shop and Maningrida was another seven or eight hours drive through the bush.

"You would live in Maningrida; base yourself at the Community Education Centre under a Principal called John Rattigan, but teach kids in outstation schools."

"I'll take it!" I said, and hung up to look for a map of the Territory. There it was on the eastern bank of the Liverpool River, about half way along the coast from Darwin on the way to Gove. I went to talk with my colleagues, leaving the boss, Bill, till last.

"Great fishing," said Monk "but Bill will be pissed off."

"Great fishing," said Ron. "Just avoid Bill for a few days."

"You mongrel, you've only been back six months and now I've got to find a replacement biology teacher," said Bill in more colourful words than that, "but you'll like the fishing."

I had several phone conversations with the Principal, John Rattigan, in the weeks before the end of the term and the four week dry season holiday. He gave me a list of things to do in Darwin before I went bush and using this list I started a bush-order account with a Darwin supermarket called Rite Price, opened accounts with Barge Express and Arnhem Air - the major transport companies servicing Maningrida - and made sure my cheque account was working so I could pay them.

There was a phone and fax at the school, one of the few in the community as they had yet to install enough lines for private houses. I could fax in a food order to Rite Price to buy what I wanted and the bush-order lady, Janet, would push the trolley around the aisles for me. Teachers in remote communities were given a freight allowance so they could buy perishable foods from Darwin and have them flown in weekly at department expense. Even my dog, Turkey, could get frozen meat flown in and the Government would pay the transport!

Barge Express used large ocean going drive-aboard freight barges that could lower a bow door to concrete beach landings and allow access. The barges arrived in Maningrida fortnightly and would bring anything you needed, from school supplies and food, to cars, boats and beer – a maximum of two cartons a fortnight if you had a 'license' from the Maningrida Council.

The school had made a booking for me on an Arnhem Air passenger flight early on a Wednesday morning. The Arnhem Air departure lounge was a tin shed well removed from the regular airport. It was both a hangar and office and several planes could be seen through the open door behind the counter. The office was small and after the check in there was a bench outside the door for passengers to wait on.

A cyclone wire fence with a combination lock gate separated us from the planes until they were ready. There was a couple of returning teachers already waiting on the bench going back for their third year in Maningrida who spoke of how wonderful the kids were and how good the fishing was. Actually they spoke mainly about the fishing and it seemed this was to be an on-going theme of life in Maningrida.

Arnhem Air was run by an enormously fat man named Ozzie, and his wife, who had been in the aviation game for many years. Ozzie was a pilot of great experience but age and health had caught up with him and he rarely flew by the time I knew him. His planes at Arnhem Air were ten seaters and there were no regulations in those days about dogs having to be in boxes or anything. Ozzie just grunted when he saw that my dog was with me and said he would be allowed to sit on the floor of the plane during the flight. Turkey was only too happy to be going anywhere at all and after we boarded was only slightly intimidated by the big goofy wolf hound dog behind him in the aisle. This dog made his presence felt regularly throughout the flight by farting long and loud. There aren't any windows you can open in these planes…

"What's that?" asked the bloke next to me pointing at Turkey with his chin.

"That's my hunting dog."

"But it's a… poodle!"

Turkey was the survivor of a broken relationship with an English woman who had returned to England, leaving me with the dog. He was a scruffy bright-eyed terrier crossed with a poodle. With his crooked little teeth, floppy ears and woolly hair the vet called "apricot" he was unique to say the least - a little pampered pooch with funny teeth in an under bite, and a sad droopy moustache.

"Great start," I thought.

The plane circled Maningrida before we landed and we had a great view of the community from the air. There were about a hundred buildings, including the houses, laid out in neat rows in a large triangle pressed against a beach. The sports oval and school were easily identifiable and the large square building had to be the shop. A barge landing dissected the beach and I could see someone unloading a small boat from his trailer into the sea.

John Rattigan was tall and impeccably dressed, with long sleeved shirts neatly buttoned at the wrists and wearing a broad brimmed hat as protection against the sun. I could tell he was a confirmed large dog guy when he eyed Turkey suspiciously as we walked across the tarmac from the plane. He gave me a quick tour of the town before dropping me off at my assigned house and telling me that plans had changed: I was now a grade 1-2 classroom teacher at the main school, not in the outstation section at all. The class was a mixed transition to grade 2 class for kids who spoke English and "other languages." The other languages were mostly Burarra, with a few speakers of Djinang and Rembarrnga thrown in for good measure. John was wary about sending a grade 12 biology teacher out to the homelands and perhaps seeing Turkey had given him cause to wonder.

"The kids range from five years to about eight" he said, "and don't worry, I bought you a book to read about teaching little kids."

What the heck? I was a bit annoyed but he had a compelling argument. Nothing in my past had prepared me for outstation teaching – who did I think I was? Anyway, I was there already so I'd read the book and give it a go.

Maningrida in mid dry season in 1989 was a dusty collection of houses split into various *camps*. First impressions after arriving at the airport included visions of piles of garbage, kids on bikes, tin shacks erected between rows of houses which were deeply stained with the red dust from the roads, and were almost invariably missing louvers from windows and decorated with graffiti. Groups of people with skin the colour of the night sat drinking tea around small cooking fires outside the houses, or in circles around a bed sheet in the shade playing cards, their toddlers running around them naked and free. Skinny dogs with large bald patches of weathered grey skin lounged around scratching at their ears enthusiastically or casually shredding disposable nappies.

The main road into Maningrida ran past the airport, down through 'Top Camp' past the town hall, the *hasty tasty* takeaway food outlet, and the Community Education Centre – a rather grand name for the school.

The school was in central Maningrida and consisted of a cluster of aging classroom buildings in three rows, with a separate office demountable and staffroom, a dark and dingy manual arts building, and a large and fairly new double pre-school next to a basketball court. One of the buildings was elevated, with two large classrooms and a staff room above a caged area. This was the high school building, not just because it was on stilts, but also because this was where the high school aged students attended classes. In the yard there were a few large trees, mainly *Melina* already dropping their yellow plum-sized fruit, but little else in terms of garden. I asked John why there wasn't more.

He shrugged. "We plant things but the sniffers pull them out the same day."

"The *sniffers*?"

"Young men, mainly, who get high on petrol. You'll see them wandering around with a can of petrol held to their noses. We have a real problem with them. They're mostly kids who should be at school, teenagers, getting high on the fumes and running wild every night. The school really needs a fence."

I thought of the irony of building a fence to keep out kids who should be in school but he had a point. I was to learn how the school verandahs were a major hang out for kids who sniffed petrol. The concrete of the verandahs was permanently marked by kids rubbing the tops off the cans. (Petrol sniffing, by the way, was stopped overnight in Maningrida about a year later when the council began to sell avgas aviation fuel, rather than petrol, because it doesn't have the same effect when inhaled.)

The school neighboured the Maningrida Council,

the Bawinanga Aboriginal Corporation (BAC) and the Maningrida Progress Association (MPA). The bulk of the community, in three housing camps, radiated out from the centre.

Top Camp, which John had already shown me as we came down from the airport, was three rows of a dozen or so houses that ran south up the gentle slope from the school and town hall area to the ruins of an old sawmill. The houses were mainly assigned and rented to Burarra people whose homelands were east along the coast around the Blyth River and Cape Stewart area. A few Nakara people, whose country lay west of the Blyth River mouth, and some Wulaki people from the other side of the Blyth River but inland from the coast, also lived here. Right at the top on the corner was the sole *Balanda*, or European, residence in this camp. Europeans in Arnhem Land are known as *Balanda*, in an interesting linguistic connection to Indonesia and the Malay language. Indonesians still call the Dutch Balanda, from the word *Hollander*. This lonely Balanda house in Top Camp belonged to the council mechanic who lived there with his pretty Thai wife, Pai, who seemed to have a perpetually stunned expression on her face.

Burarra and Wulaki people always appeared to get along well and there were many inter-tribal marriages among them. Quite a few were relatively well educated and, as I got to know them, they appeared sophisticated in a western sense but still maintained strong traditional values.

Beside the school was a large oval for community

football matches and on its far side was 'Side Camp'. This was a small group of houses and a number of *cages* – roofs with wire walls for security. This camp seemed to act as a reception area for *bushies* from the western Maningrida area, as here stayed people from the Kunwinjku, Goregone, Koln, or Rembarrnga tribes. These families would often come to Maningrida from the outstations for shopping or ceremony or to sit out the wet season, so there were often sizeable population shifts.

The third camp was a little way along the coast. Known as 'Bottom Camp', this was the home of the Kunavidji landowners for the Maningrida township area and it seemed to be a bit of a princedom in its own right. It was separated as much by the short stretch of bush between it and the rest of Maningrida as it appeared to be by attitude. The Kunavidji were the landowners and everyone knew we were only here with their permission because among their number were a few loud drunks who'd make sure they'd tell you whenever they could.

At school the Kunavidjis had their own bilingual program but their primary classes were renowned for being the wildest kids and most difficult to teach in the school. In the time I lived in Maningrida I saw many teachers exhausted trying to run their classes. I took a Kunavidji class only once to relieve Lina Penna, the regular teacher who was away in Darwin for the day.

"Don't take them outside!" Lina warned.

But I forgot her advice – they were a great bunch of kids and we had an excellent first lesson in the classroom. "They're easy," I thought. "What are people complaining about?"

The next lesson they were supposed to be mapping the school as a maths activity. How can you do that without going outside? We needed to pace out how long buildings were and estimate their size in relation to each other, and draw a map showing their location on a large sheet of cardboard, so outside we went. Within five minutes I was almost alone. Kids ran everywhere, some went back home, some just played. They were used to having complete autonomy and they made the most of it. I shouted and cajoled and pleaded with them but there was no way I could do any teaching and there was nothing I could do to bring them back into the classroom. I didn't have enough energy to return to the classroom to draw the map all by myself.

"Told you so," said Lina on her return.

I lived in another side camp to the east but I don't remember it ever having a name like the other parts of town. It was across two large fields from the school, which in earlier days were a banana plantation but were now used for touch footy and soccer games. Many of the hundred or so Balanda who lived in Maningrida community had their houses in this part of town. Here there were the nurses' quarters, the police station, teachers and other government workers and community organization managers, mechanics, builders and office workers. The Aborigines living here were mostly government workers – Aboriginal health workers, teachers or council employees and there were some 'foreigners' from Milingimbi or further afield. There was even an Arranda family from central Australia.

This part of town was clearly the most westernized as many Balanda had magnificent tropical gardens, and expensive boats parked on trailers in their yards with lawn sprinklers shooting out gallons of bore water. Giant African mahogany trees shaded some of the houses and Carpentaria palms, frangipani, mango, rambutan and cashew trees were common behind the neat two meter high fences which delineated the boundaries. The sweet scent of the frangipani flowers and the clicking of garden sprinklers meant parts of this camp were more like a suburb of Darwin than a bush community, despite the gravel roads.

In stark contrast, the houses of the locals were marked by untidy yards with long dry grass or burnt ground where grass had been thick and long in the wet season. They also had boats without trailers, broken bikes, rusting hulks of Land Cruisers and lots of hairless or mangy dogs hanging around eating whatever was thrown to them, or scratching at the ticks which hung from their ears. In July the only green areas in these yards were the long grass clumps growing around dripping taps. My first impressions were that clearly the locals had a worldview very different to my own.

John Rattigan (who I quickly discovered was always called "Johnrattigan", as if it was one word) dropped me off at a three bedroom grey brick house in 'Middle Road'. It had been vacant for a while, or at least hadn't had anyone living in it interested in cleaning or gardening. The linoleum floor was stained red with the dust from outside and it was sparsely furnished. In the living room and kitchen there was a cane lounge, a laminated table, four vinyl-covered steel chairs and a large fridge and a chest freezer. Each bedroom had a bed with a stained mattress and built in wardrobes and there was an old chipboard dresser, which at some time had been wet and the chipboard had swollen in parts. The louver windows were caged with small gauge security mesh but the louvers were so dirty I had to open them to see out. The bathroom looked like a science experiment on the best conditions in which to grow mould and fungi.

I spent three days cleaning and preparing the house before my gear was due to arrive on the barge. The people next door had a Dolly Parton tape and they played *Jolene* and *Coat of Many Colours* at full volume so many times in those three days I still know all the words. Along with the music, and the quick realization that as a single teacher I'd soon be sharing my three bedroom house, when I was offered a one bedroom donga on the next road I jumped at the chance and moved in there. Home for the next five and a half years, it was merely two rooms plus a bathroom and a laundry. It wasn't air conditioned and was pretty run down but it was mine – I loved living there and I spent many weekends working on the garden. It was a little hot box in the wet season – when it was really hot I'd get up several times during the night and have a cold shower then go back to bed wet with the ceiling fan on maximum above me. I cooled it one year by running fine mist sprinklers into the trees above it to keep the tin roof permanently wet and inside the temperature dropped four or five degrees. The next year I put an electric air conditioner into the wall which kept it 20 degrees cooler.

A *Barge Express* ship arrived at the barge landing once a week to deliver all the goods necessary for the town. We used to take turns at "barge duty" and because the boat came with the tide, it could mean getting up in the small hours of the night to unload school supplies from bright yellow ten foot shipping containers into the school Land Cruisers for delivery to the school and teachers' houses. Anyone in Maningrida who ordered goods from Darwin would need to be there to unload their goods, so it was often a social occasion and, indeed, it was one of the first opportunities a new chum like me got to meet many of the non-Aboriginal members of the community who worked outside of the school – council workers, service providers, builders and others.

I was there the night my stuff was arriving. Chris Baldwin, an assistant Principal of the school, picked me up about midnight and we went to the barge landing. The barge, inexplicably named after the English queen who lasted only nine days, *The Lady Jane*, was brightly lit and noisy. Her giant screws churned the water behind her so she was pushed constantly against the concrete and a large forklift truck was already unloading the containers. One of them contained all my worldly goods.

Chris and I walked up the ship's ramp and climbed

up to the bridge. Here we met some of the crew and collected manifest lists for all the stuff we had to pick up. For a while we chatted to the captain, who was happy to tell a story of one of the barge company guys, George, who had landed in trouble. It's probably a tall story but we all had a good laugh anyway: In his back yard in Darwin George had had a pet crocodile which had grown quite large. He used to feed it chickens and, apparently, it was quite a passive beast, but one day it killed the neighbour's cat, though when it was discovered it hadn't yet eaten it.

"So what do you do with a dead cat?" asked the captain. "Obviously you want to hide the evidence, so George thought as it was dead already, better that the crocodile finish eating it. So there he was pushing the bloody cat into the croc's mouth when the neighbour popped his head over the fence and said, 'Have you seen my cat?'." He laughed. "Try to get out of that one!"

Chris took his manifests down to the dock and organized for the forklift driver to drop off my container at my house for unpacking. We then spent several hours loading school supplies into the Land Cruisers and driving them up to the school and around to teachers' houses. It was the first barge of the school term and there were hundreds of items. The pile of juice boxes in the school canteen towered over my head and the first light of dawn was breaking in the east by the time we'd finished.

On the first day of school it became evident to me that my confidence as a primary school teacher may have been a little misplaced. I really had no idea how to teach five year olds and it was with no small trepidation that I met with the kids. I knew that they had had a proper teacher the semester before and the teacher assistant, Jimmy Gularawuna, was an old hand. So I reckoned that even if I managed to fool the kids, Jimmy was sure to catch me out as a fraud.

I thought honesty was the best policy, as it usually is with kids. More than 20 arrived this first day and sat on the mat at my feet. I introduced myself and told them where I was from, then asked them some questions about what they had done in the holidays or where they lived. Every now and then one of them, Cain, would poke at my legs with his index finger. I ignored him for a while but eventually asked him what he was doing.

"Looking," he replied.

"At what?"

"This!" and he poked my leg again and when he pulled his finger away a small pale spot was left behind. It quickly returned to normal colour as the blood returned. Black skin doesn't do this, and watching it happen on a Balanda's skin is endless entertainment for Aboriginal kids.

We continued. They were extraordinarily polite – something I wasn't used to in a high school situation. I thought, "I *can* do this after all!"

I told them I'd never taught little kids before and asked them to help me. The rest of that day they kept me to the routine they were used to – lining up where they were supposed to, organizing their pencils in the right way or reminding me when it was maths or story time. They were a wonderful bunch of kids and over the next six months we had a great time together and I learned much, and hope they did too.

The class was designed to cater for regular attending Balanda kids in transition, grade 1 and grade 2 and it was also a reception class for Burarra visitors in from the homeland centers on the other side of the Blyth River, over 100 kilometers away. By the end of the semester there were more than 50 kids on the roll, with about 20 attending on most days. There was a core group of about ten Balanda kids and Aborigines who were being raised by Balanda families and they would come to school nearly every day.

We had a lot of fun. I found that being a primary teacher was a license to display eccentricities which I wouldn't get away with in a high school. For example, teaching backwards counting from one hundred is always more fun if you get down to "5, 4, 3, 2, 1 Zero! Blast off!" and race around the room making rocket noises. Teenagers just think you're an idiot!

One day a Black Hawk helicopter landed on the oval next to the school to pick up a couple of *Norforce* soldiers for reserve army training. Of course every kid in the school raced out and crushed each other against the fence to get the best view. I joined them and saw a tall elderly Colonel alight from the aircraft and walk slowly across the field. Without thinking I leapt the fence and bore down on him:

"Oy!" I shouted above the noise. "You can't park there!"

The officer blinked in surprise. "Err… I beg your pardon?"

"I said you can't park there. There's a parking fee."

"Oh… I see. What do you mean?" We were now eye to eye – which at two meters tall is a rare event for me.

"There's a toll. You have to show the kids your helicopter!"

"Ah, yes of course," he said. He turned to the pilot and told him to organize the kids and soon every one of them, in groups of five, was allowed to climb in and explore the helicopter and play for a few minutes.

"Thanks, mate. Welcome," I said offering my hand. "Derek Pugh – nice to meet you."

"No problem, our pleasure," he replied smiling, gripping my hand with surprising strength. "Austin Asche. Glad to be here."

If I'd known that the tall Colonel arriving by helicopter was *The Honourable* Sir Justice Austin Asche, AC, QC, the Northern Territory's thirteenth Administrator and Queen's representative, war hero and Companion of the Order of Australia, I would perhaps have shown a little more respect. Sometimes I can lodge my size 12 foot firmly in my mouth, but I was lucky he had a sense of humour, and the kids had a great learning experience. They wrote stories about it afterwards, which I posted to the honourable Colonel for posterity's sake. I told the kids he would most likely stick them on the fridge door in Admiralty House with vice regal magnets. He sent back a nice note thanking the kids for their stories.

The classroom assistant teacher, Jimmy Gularawu-na, knew who he was of course, and teased me mercilessly about it afterwards. He knew everyone and like most Arnhem Landers, never forgot a face. He was born at Cape Don in 1939 so when we worked together he was in his fifties, and thus a tribal elder. In the 1950s he was one of the Arnhem Land Aborigines I write about in chapter 12 who so worried the Government after World War 2, when they drifted to town camps in Darwin where there was very poor infrastructure with which to support them. Jimmy was 11 years old when he left his mother and first walked to Darwin with a man called Jacky Ungulbu. It was a walk of more than 320 kilometers and required living off the land on the way. He talked about it with fond memories, but I knew that such a walk must have been fraught with many difficulties - crocodiles at every river crossing for one.

In Darwin Jimmy went to a 'welfare school' and learned to read and write and the "European ways of living" but he said he missed his mother and returned to Milingimbi and then the Blyth River to see her when the opportunity of a free boat ride arose. This came in the form of a Welfare Department boat when they tried to relieve some of the pressure in Darwin. And pressure there was: people were arriving from all over the Top End bush in their hundreds and, perhaps weakened from their journey or their new life in "the long grass", they ended up trapped there until someone else provided transport back home.

Jimmy spent a year or two back in the bush with his family but in 1959 his mate, Tommy Wadaminya, talked him into starting the long walk back to Darwin once more and they set off from the Blyth River. Within days they'd reached the area around Maningrida and ran into Dave Drysdale, who Jimmy recognized from the welfare school in the city. Literate people were few and far between and Drysdale asked Jimmy if he would help Mrs Drysdale work at the leprosarium she had set up, which he agreed to. Although he said the work was very hard, he stayed for a couple of years before continuing his walk into Darwin. This time he found a job working with the army and later the navy where he had several different roles, including at one time a job in a meat works.

Jimmy returned to Maningrida in 1968 and again became a health worker at the hospital. When I lived in Maningrida there were a few people around who still called him "Dr Jimmy." He worked there for a few years until Ji-marda Outstation School opened in the mid 1970s and he was recruited to be its first teacher. He ran the school for nine years before transferring to Maningrida to work as assistant in the mixed grade 1 and 2 class and he was lumbered with me, a high school biology teacher pretending to be a primary teacher, in 1989.

Jimmy had an adventurous spirit, even taking a package tour by himself to Bali one year. A few years after I left Maningrida, he retired and went to live with relatives in Darwin. I ran into him a couple of times in Casuarina Mall and we'd have a cappuccino or two and it was always good to see him. He passed away a while later after a career of many years as a health worker and teaching or assisting in schools. As an elder he was a true link between western and traditional culture and he taught me much.

I was proud to have known Jimmy and because we got on well he 'gave' me his name and skin name. So, to everyone, I also became *Gularawuna*, skin name *Gela* or *Burralang*, moiety *Dhuwa*, named by a Burarra elder from Point Stewart country out past Yilan and Ji-marda.

Skin names are incredibly important to Aboriginal people in the Top End and they give their owner an identity. Once mine was known, people I'd just met would be able to pigeon hole me and know how they related. They would tell me:

"That one is your mother (*Bangardijan*), your brother (another *Gela*). Here's *Bulanjan* your *kalekale* (darling)."

The women who are *Bulanjan* or *Narichjan* are in the correct marriage groups for all Gela men (although Narichjan was also our maternal grandmothers' group). Various other names or titles could be used to address me. For example, I was always called *Anjerro* by Gordon Machbirrbirr, another Gela, and thus my brother. Some of the kids would address me as son, or uncle, depending on our relationships.

Every living thing in the Aboriginal world is divided into two groups called moieties. In Arnhem Land the names of these moieties are *Dhuwa* and *Yirritja*. All Gela men belong to the Dhuwa moiety for example but other groups were Yirritja. Because everyone is believed to derive from a range of totemic beings, or spiritual ancestors, their moiety is a direct reference to which beings and which creation story they might be 'owners' of. Plants and animals belong to the moieties just as strongly. For example, barramundi and red apple trees are *Yirritja* whilst emus and agile wallabies are *Dhuwa*. The result is that there are foods, or parts of them at least, which individuals are not allowed to eat.

I was told that as a Dhuwa man, when I die I will be taken over the sea in a spirit canoe early one morning, traveling on the light cast by the morning star, which is kind of appealing.

Membership of a moiety meant other rules too. One day I was driving though a part of the country where there was some 'secret business' happening. I was stopped by a group of men who asked who I was and which moiety I was in. I was lucky: if I'd been a Yirritja man I'd have been in serious trouble as Yirritja men were not allowed to drive in that area during the business. I have heard of people being levied serious 'fines' of many hundreds of dollars for breaking rules like this.

At the end of the semester it seemed I had proved myself enough for a reassignment to an outstation teaching job. Johnrattigan came to see me just before the Christmas break.

"Are you still interested in working in the outstations?" he asked.

"Of course," I replied.

"We're expanding in that direction. You can be the third teacher in the unit. Have a good holiday."

Wow! I didn't need a holiday, I was ready then and there, but reason prevailed and I used some of the six week holiday to prepare. I bought a large swag (a canvas covered bedroll), a mosquito net and a new hat and, without really knowing what to expect turned up on the first day of the new school year raring to go.

The weather beat me back. It was the height of the wet season and a cyclone was passing to the north. A few days of heavy rain kept me huddled in the outstation's office building writing teaching programs for kids I had never met. In the second week of term, though, I loaded everything into a small plane and headed off to the Kunwinjku homeland centre called Marrkolidjban.

2
KUNWINJKU

In 1990 Maningrida Community Education Centre ran seven outstation schools with another two on a temporary hiatus. The two other visiting teachers were already experienced in the job: Murray Garde, a Queenslander with a phenomenal ability to learn new languages, and Zoe Morgan, a resourceful farm girl with endless patience for working with small children.

Murray worked with the Kunwinjku outstations – Marrkolidjban, Mumeka and Yikarrakkal. Zoe looked after four Rembarrnga outstation schools for the tribe who came from the edge of the Stone Country. These communities were inland, almost directly south of Maningrida and delightfully named Borlkdjam, Buluhkaduru, Kolorbidahdah and Mankorlod. Some of these were tough names for a new chum like me to learn to say correctly, so I was always glad we didn't run schools at Barnamarrakkakanora or Nabbarlakunindabba.

Murray and I decided that we would share teaching at Marrkolidjban because of the high

Me, with teacher Geoffrey Campion and the Outstations Sports Team
which travelled to Gapuwiyak to compete in 1992.

numbers of kids there, and that we'd teach there
in alternate weeks. The weeks when Murray was
at Marrkolidjban would see me travelling east to
Ji-marda and Yilan in the Burarra lands on the
other side of the Blyth River. I went initially by
plane but, as the roads dried out, by 130 kilometers
of track through the forest in a school Land Cruiser.
The Burarra schools had needed little attention for
a year or more as few people had been living in
the outstations but now the children were back
and they wanted the schools to run again. Having
been given Jimmy Gularawuna's name I was
already considered a 'Burarra Balanda' by many
people so this worked out well.

Murray was a veteran of outstation education and had worked in them for several years. He could speak Kunwinjku fluently and later even wrote a dictionary of the language and trained in anthropology to become Dr Garde, now a noted researcher and advocate for Aborigines. The men at Marrkolidjban told me he had learned their language "right through" in six weeks. When I was teaching at Marrkolidjban Murray would travel to Mumeka and Yikarrakkal to support those schools.

Marrkolidjban was a cluster of tin roofed humpies and three or four tin sheds spread over four or five hundred square meters at the northern end of a bush airstrip. The people generally lived outside around their fire places and they built stick platforms with corrugated iron shelves upon which they could put their food and provisions, above the reach of their dogs and a mob of semi-tame pigs that ran around the outstation with impunity.

There were still some trees growing among the houses –mainly the introduced *Melina*, a few stringy-barks and woollybutts plus a couple of mango and cashew trees, but much of the ground was picked clean of vegetation, which was then swept into side areas with the rubbish, and burned. This kept the snakes away from the living area and marked where the kids could wander around safely at night.

Marrkolidjban Outstation School was a square tin shed, walled on two sides and open on the others, but with a heavy mesh fence and a gate to keep the dogs and pigs out. It was designed and built a few years earlier as part of a set and most of the other schools serviced by Maningrida in those days used the same design. The school furniture consisted of two giant picnic style tables and a lockable corner room which housed the school supplies and the radio.

The Marrkolidjban people, as I have said, are of the Kunwinjku tribe and their outstation is on the eastern edge of their tribal lands. Kunwinjku land stretches from the upper Liverpool River nearly through to Gunbalanya and Kakadu on the East Alligator River.

Marrkolidjban was always the biggest home-land school serviced from Maningrida in terms of numbers, with up to 35 children attending. All the outstation kids studied a self paced program officially called 'School of the Bush' but which we called the *Bushbooks*. This was limited but multi level and students could use them with the teacher assistants who would run the schools when the visiting teachers were not there. The visiting teachers' roles were to expand on the program and ensure adequate English literacy and numeracy was delivered.

I worked all that year at Marrkolidjban but in 1991 we managed to arrange for a teacher to visit every week exclusively because of the large numbers of kids, and this seemed to suit the community well. Having a visiting teacher every week was until then unheard of in Maningrida outstation schools and, in fact, it meant Marrkolidjban had qualified as a single-teacher school, except that it continued to be serviced by a visiting teacher. (Gochan Jiny-Jirra School, which was smaller and only 30 minutes drive from Maningrida, continued to be a single-teacher school, with a teacher living in the community).

Alan Schroeder, an older guy originally from Canada but with many years experience in a number of Aboriginal communities, was recruited to take over this school as his only visiting teacher destination. Alan was an unusual man, and what he thought of us young blokes and the pranks we sometimes played on him I never found out.

Alan was a lover of ice cream. He'd bring 20 buckets of the stuff in from Darwin and store them in our school freezer. Sometimes the temptation was too much to bear. If Alan was out bush Murray and I would eat the top centimeter out of a can, then melt the surface so it would freeze again without leaving spoon marks, and put it back in the freezer. Alan never said anything and I, of course, blame Murray.

When I first started at Marrkolidjban it took but a day to teach me that I was in a different league to Murray when it came to learning language. I sat down with a young couple on my first evening there. Charlie Trevallen and Margot, whose kids attended the school already, were a devoted couple and they and their three beautiful children quickly became friends. Their continuous good humour and friendly welcomes made visits easy. They were highly traditional people intent on keeping their culture strong and Charlie was ritualistically scarred across his chest and arms with the raised scars he had earned in ceremonies. On my first night they gave me a language lesson. A dozen others drifted over to listen and offer advice.

Charlie started by getting me to write down the words he told me: *gamak* and *maynmak*, both meaning good; *wurdurt*, children; *wodemrai*, come here; *muful*, mouse.

Pronunciation was my first hurdle and I crashed and burned. Soon a crowd had gathered and people all around me were rolling around holding their sides with laughter. When I heard people say *"muful"* they actually said *"mupul"* as there is no 'f' sound in the Kunwinjku language.

I tried again, and sounded like a demented cow, *"mooofooool."*

Twenty people corrected me. *"Mupul, mupul."*

"Muful" I mimicked to roars of laughter.

I gave up for the evening, discouraged by my lack of an ear for their language.

My swag was in the school so I headed to bed with Turkey the dog for company. As I drifted off to sleep I could hear the young men going over and over my language lesson:

"Muful, muful," then more great peals of laughter. I knew that no one was going to boast that I had learned their language "right through" in six weeks.

The kids at Marrkolidjban were a marvelous happy, smiling bunch who would welcome the teacher's arrival enthusiastically each visit and would throw themselves into school activities with gusto.

The community provided two women, Barbara Namundja and Louise Dinguwanga, to work as teacher assistants in the school and both had worked there for several years before my arrival. Variously called teacher assistants, assistant teachers or Aboriginal teachers, they would sometimes be the only people who had regular jobs in the homelands. Their pay was low, in fact less than the dole if they had dependents, but they took a real pride in their status. It was their job to teach the kids when the visiting teacher was away in Maningrida or at other schools and to help the teacher when he or she was visiting. Some had very low literacy levels, but the success of the school depended on them and most were external students, studying to be teachers through Batchelor College, a large college based in the town of Batchelor, just south of Darwin. To help them we ran a radio reading program, where each child would read to one of the visiting teachers on duty in the radio room back in Maningrida. The program usually ran something like this:

"Victor Zulu 8 Maningrida School calling Marrkolidjban Outstation. Is there anyone there to read today?" *crackle crackle, wait...* Barbara would come on line.

"Yo, good morning, Derek, yes, here Sonya."

"Good morning, Sonya"

"Good morning, Derek" was the bright high pitched reply.

"What are you reading today, Sonya?"

And then the monotone of young children reading amid the crackle of static, often with the whispers of the TAs helping out in the background:

"Micky has a ball...... Jacinta has a doll...... Father has a billy can... "

On and on the reading went for more than 120 kids each morning. It was a valuable program but by golly it was boring! The teachers took it in turns, so once every four weeks we'd have to stay in Maningrida for 'radio duty'. Nobody ever looked forward to it. It was so boring that Murray and I used to entertain ourselves by writing and illustrating our own versions of the *Bushbook* stories while we listened to the kids read the real ones. They were never likely to be published:

"Micky has a hernia...... Jacinta has a nubbin...... Father has a prolapsed bowel... "

Barbara had a young baby and she would breast feed him whilst teaching in the school. She usually wore a singlet so she could hoist a breast out an armhole and her baby could feed easily. She'd change breasts and forget the first one was still out and even sometimes forget the second. So on more than one occasion I'd have the odd spectacle of a woman teaching a group of young kids with both breasts hooked out of her singlet, the baby asleep on the floor.

Clothing was sometimes a bit of an issue for the young kids at Marrkolidjban because we used to insist they wear at least pants to school, but often had to settle with underpants for many of them. The state of dress and cleanliness of clothing was irrelevant, because actually coming to school was the important thing. We did not want the situation I found years later in Pularumpi where kids would not come to school because they didn't have clean clothes and it was a 'shame job'.

There were always tiny kids, actually too young

for school, but who would hang around, and they'd invariably be naked. One day there was a toddler of about two in the school standing on the table. I was teaching at the other table when,

Ppphhlllttt!!!

I turned to see that projectile diarrhoea had sprayed neatly across the pages of an exercise book a 12 year old named Jeremy was working in. Jeremy hardly blinked. He folded the pages up, tore them out of his book and dropped them over the wall near him, where they were quickly eaten by dogs. One of the kids took the toddler outside to hose him down and the class went on.

The second assistant teacher at the school was Louise. Stout and stern faced, she always carried herself with dignity and I never saw her get angry or upset at anything. Her son was Elijah, about seven years old with a number 11 of snot perpetually on his top lip and wild curly hair. He was a nice kid but one day he didn't come into school and we could see him playing around the houses. That afternoon after school I was running an art activity and Elijah turned up and wanted to join in. I said no, he hadn't come to school so he would miss out. The tantrum he turned on then was a spectacularly memorable performance - he screamed and kicked and shouted abuse for 10 minutes or more. Louise just looked at me and said

"Next time you will know!"

Elijah forgave me in time. One day he gave me a big kiss on the cheek, and in my mind's eye I can still see the strands of snot that connected my beard with his retreating nose.

Dogs are ubiquitous in Aboriginal communities. They are greatly loved but it's very much survival of the fittest, because they are not usually pampered pets. The dogs in outstations were often infested with ticks and fleas, and many were hairless with skin infections. Every now and then there'd be a plague of ticks and it'd be hard to see where ticks stopped and dogs started and lots of dogs would die during these times.

There were always loads of puppies around and the kids would play with them for hours. They'd get the puppies to suckle on their fingers and sometimes on their outward protruding belly buttons.

One day just after dawn I was in my swag at Marrkolidjban and enjoying the cool and the unusual fog that had enveloped us. Out of the gloom a toddler passed by with a puppy. He held it by its front legs and it lay quietly, slung over his shoulder. Another puppy was jumping up to the first and clearly annoying the boy.

"*Whack!*" the boy clubbed the jumping puppy with what was most easily at hand – the other puppy, then swung it back over his shoulder again. Neither puppy seemed surprised or injured by the incident.

Marrkolidjban was rather unusual for outstations because they also had a mob of about a dozen pigs living as pets among the houses. The dogs and pigs would compete for food and sometimes the dogs would chase them off. Once during school a pig ran past squealing loudly with a dog firmly attached to his tail. It escaped when the entire skin of its tail peeled off and the dog settled down to his unexpected meal.

The pigs could be quite a distraction to school lessons. One morning a sow was being mounted by two boars. Pigs have a corkscrew like penis which hunts out its target during intercourse as if with a mind of its own. On this occasion, much entertainment and hours of giggling arose after the second boar's hole seeking erection discovered the wrong hole, resulting in the first boar squealing in indignation and then turning sharply with bulging eyes to bite the intruder savagely on his snout. Try teaching kids a maths lesson during that!

A few years after I'd left Maningrida I was living in Darwin. Murray Garde, then working for the Djomi Museum in Maningrida, asked me to be the photographer on a music collecting expedition to Mumeka, a neighbouring Kunwinjku community on the Mann River some 25 kilometers from Marrkolidjban. A sound recordist and he were planning to document a collection of Kunwinjku songs performed by a song man named Kevin Djimarr, with a didgeridoo accompaniment by Owen Yalandja, a very large softly spoken man with an extraordinarily full beard.

I drove out from Darwin to Maningrida and picked Murray up and together we headed out to Mumeka. Murray found a long forgotten bottle of wine I'd had under a seat for several months and together we polished it off despite its foul vinegar taste and, singing at the tops of our voices, we headed west into a fiery sunset.

Because of, or in spite of, the wine we arrived at Mumeka well after dark. A large number of people were sitting around camp fires and when we joined a group Murray introduced me. Many people vaguely remembered me from my days at Marrkol-idjban but when they were heard that I was *Gela* with Burarra connections, they immediately knew exactly who I was, relaxed and introduced them-selves in kin relationship terms. All I could see in the dark were white teeth and glinting eyes so I remembered no names the next morning. It was a night of revelry though, and all the kids and the young men and girls daubed themselves with white clay, built up the fires for light and danced the night away to the rhythmic didge and clap sticks.

The Mumeka people were incredibly hospitable and it was a joy to visit them. We spent a couple of days collecting and recording their songs. Murray wrote them down and translated them – a not insig-nificant task, but made easier by the fact that Kun-winjku songs are short and repetitive. For the record-ing we moved for the day out of the noisy community and based ourselves in the middle of a floodplain so the recordings include a background chorus of the screeches of corellas and red tailed black cockatoos in the distance.

Manih wanjh kun-wok manbu kah-wayini:
Ngune-re Ngalmadjenge mandjarduk ngune-rikan
ngune-re Ngalmadjenge mandjarduk ngune-rikan

ngune-re Ngalmadjenge
nangaleh nuye
Nakakkak nuye
ngune-re ngune-mang
ngunem-kan ngune-won
ngune-won ka-baye

You go with your niece [who is my grandmother]
and go and get red apple fruit (repeated)
Whose is it?
It is for your mother's mother's brother [and the
one I call uncle]
You both go and get it
Bring it here and give it to him
Give it to him to bite
(from *Wurrurrumi Kun-Borrk*, Kevin Djimarr)

Murray has spent many years working at Mumeka
as a teacher and visiting in his later careers. He had
met Jon Altman who had done some anthropologi-
cal work at Mumeka years before and written books
and papers on a wide range of things from child
rearing practices to economics in the outstations.
Murray tells the story about sitting around a fire at
Mumeka and saying to the crowd:

"Oh, and by the way Jon Altman says to say
hello."

And obediently, from around the circle, came the
chorus "hello."

3

BURARRA

Every second week I'd travel west of Maningrida to visit the long established outstation schools of Ji-marda and Yilan. Both these schools had been dormant for a year or so, but people were now living more permanently at them and wanted the schools to start up again in earnest. In the beginning because of wet season the only access was by plane. These communities were east of the mouth of the Blyth River; Yilan was on the beach and Ji-marda was a little inland. Ji-marda was a particularly good place if any entomologist wanted to study mosquitoes. Mosquitoes were one of the major totems of the area and at certain times and tides the air was thick with them. There's a dance people from here do where they squat and slap themselves to the beat of the clapsticks – the mosquito squashing dance.

Ji-marda had an airstrip and was a small cluster of humpies and a house or two on the southern side of the airstrip. Years before the dwellings had been on the northern side and the school still stood there

Ji-Malawa School started on a tarpaulin. After several months we installed a garden shed and a small roof to be the school.

in its original position now hidden among the spear grass and regrowth from the forest. It was another version of the open shed found at Marrkolidjban but being hundreds of meters from the nearest house proved a lonely place to camp so I rarely spent the night here. The only advantage to staying was a wind-mill close by where I set up a bath tub in which I could lounge around for hours by myself on a hot afternoon.

Ji-marda was more associated with the mouth of the Blyth River rather than the beach only a couple of kilometers north. It was physically separated from the beach and Yilan Outstation by a swamp of reeds on the northern side and its houses seemed to be pressed against the airstrip from the south by a thin swathe of monsoon rain forest that opened up on its further side to wide grasslands and black soil plains.

Ji-marda's leaders were people like Charles Godjirra who became reasonably well known politically at some point, and there were a number of elderly men who lived there permanently. I had the impression that Ji-marda was becoming the homeland you returned to in your dotage to wait for death. Old Benny was one such bloke.

I knew Benny from my first months in Maningrida. He was an entertaining old man with lots of stories, and as the father of my 'skin brother' Gordon Machbirrbirr, who worked at the school, he was my father too and sometimes would drop in early in the morning for breakfast. Gordon told me that Benny had powerful magic and that he was a senior law man for the Burarra tribe. He had two stones he could magically send anywhere in the world to execute people, and Gordon could actually name people who had died through their use.

Benny returned to Ji-marda to die, and the last few months of his life were spent lying under a mosquito net. I'd sit and drink tea with him in his last days and could barely see him through the dark green net, but occasionally one skinny hand would emerge from under it to take up his mug or scratch Turkey's ear, and he'd sit and talk quietly, happy that he was in his country. His funeral was a major event with people coming long distances to pay their respects.

Yilan, like Ji-marda was a Burarra homeland centre. The people here lived closer to the beach, actually in the dunes, about three kilometers across the swamp north of Ji-marda. To get there in the wet season I'd fly to Ji-marda and walk through the swamp, knee deep in water, carrying all my school supplies, my swag and food for the week, with Turkey the dog swimming along behind me. In my first year of visiting I usually slept at Yilan School when I visited the Burarra side, because the mosquitoes were kinder. Even so I remember nights when everyone in the community would be sheltering under their nets as soon as it got dark, sweating in the hot and breathless night air waiting for sleep and listening to the all-pervading hum of the blanket of mosquitoes which had descended on the community. I couldn't even read by torchlight on these nights because of a myriad of tiny insects that would force themselves through the net to get to the light and then stick to the sweat on my face. Thus there were some long evenings here and sometimes I could understand the stories of one of my predecessors arriving by plane, throwing out a box of *Bushbooks* and pencils, and then taking off again in a big hurry.

One Friday I had been camping at Yilan for the week and I heard the plane approaching to collect me. I left Yilan School to meet it, setting off along the dunes, through the mangroves, into the reed swamp then up and around the grove of bush apple trees. I could see Brett through the heat shimmer. He had landed his plane and was waiting in the shade of one of the wings. It was midday, stinking hot and I was carrying a pack. I was still several hundred meters from him but I could see he was agitated, waving his arms and slapping himself but

I couldn't tell why until I walked into a wall of mosquitoes. Clouds of them descended on me, a million humming hypodermic syringes swirling in clouds, getting stuck in my sweat, darting in to harvest my life blood. I swatted one in my ear so hard I nearly knocked myself out. I was carrying a heavy pack and it was as hot as Hades, but I started running and screaming like a banshee…

"BRETT, I'M COMING… START THE ENGINE… LET'S GET OUT OF HERE!"

As a *Burarra Balanda* and because of my friendship and association with Jimmy Gularawuna from my first year in Maningrida, I quickly began to build more of an affinity with the Burarra families than I ever did with the Kunwinjku. I even started to take classes in the Burarra language and actually made some headway over the next few years. Jimmy was a Burarra elder and had spent years teaching at Jimarda School prior to his transfer to town. His country was coastal land further east on the way to Cape Stewart and as a receiver of his name it was mine too. Really! One afternoon I was driving through there hunting with some kids and I took a wrong turn. There was much shouting and I had to back up and take the other track. I clearly had much to learn. Fiona, a young girl from Wurdeja just shook her head and said,

"You should know, Derek. This is *your* country!"

As the wet season came to a close there was more movement possible between the outstations. I learnt that inland across the floodplains and grasslands there were other Burarra homeland centers in the bush along the road between Maningrida and Ji-marda: Ji-malawa, Wurdeja and Damdam. There was also a Wulaki outstation named Gamardi where they spoke a language called Djinang, which is more closely related to the Yolngu languages of the eastern Arnhem Land region than Burarra.

As the roads dried out and I could cross the rivers in a school Land Cruiser, I used to pass by Gamardi and Ji-malawa on the way to Yilan and Ji-marda. In fact, in those days the road actually went right through them. People were always very friendly and I knew many of the kids as they'd been to school at times in Maningrida and often people would stop me to hitch rides in my ute between communities.

Someone passed a message to me that the Wurdeja people were interested in opening a school and wanted to know if I would mind visiting them. However, I'd never been to either Wurdeja or its neighbour Damdam before and I had to ask the way at Gamardi the first time I was heading there.

"Just turn left at the Debil-debil Tree" said Young Michael at Gamardi.

I knew the Devil Tree. Along the track to Ji-marda in an area of thick forest was a large yellow crowned palm. These beautiful palms (*Gronophylum ramsayi*) have limited distribution in Arnhem Land. There was a forest of them near Gochan Jiny-Jirra (Cadell), but this lone tree was the only one I ever saw east of the Blyth River. It was huge, and people had a special reverence for it. They called it the

Debil-debil or Devil Tree and as we passed it many people would throw out an offering of cigarettes. The track was quite close to the tree and I could see a small pile of cigarettes had built up there over the years.

I drove past it one day on the way to Ji-marda with Jimmy Cooper. He looked into his dwindling supply of tobacco and clearly didn't want to share his remaining few cigarettes with a tree, so he lied to the devil.

"Bobo, debil," he said aloud. "Sorry. Gottim no *jambaku* today."

I asked him why people left cigarettes there at all.

"Ahh, good luck," he replied. "Make him travel no worries, no gettim accident…"

So my first visit to Wurdeja was merely a matter of taking the first left at the Debil-debil Tree and cruising through the trees until I arrived at the clearing.

The Wurdeja people are people of the forest. They speak a dialect of Burarra called *Martay Burarra,* after the orange blossoms that fall from the stringybark forests. One of the seasons of the Burarra calendar is also named after these *martay* trees and it translates as the "time when the orange blossom falls." It is an idiom for the season when you can find bush honey called *sugar bag,* made by little stingless native bees in tree hollows.

There were about twenty kids hanging around Wurdeja that day and some of the adults talked about the possibility of starting a school there. They said that two sisters, Linda and Georgina, could be the assistant teachers. It seemed a great idea to me and I asked John Rattigan to come out and talk with the community as Principal. He came the next week and was easy to convince that Wurdeja was a worthy community and with his approval I started to get some materials together and plan a new school. It was May, and dry. I consulted my visiting teacher colleagues, Zoe and Murray.

"All you need," they said "is a box of *School of the Bush* books and some maths teaching resources, a tarpaulin to put on the ground and a mobile chalk board. You can get the radio set up later."

It seemed that everywhere there were kids with no school. Damdam community was a single family outstation with a little boy named Linus, set about a kilometer away through the bush from Wurdeja. Jimalawa, with three or four families of about eight children, was around six kilometers away. All these kids would join the school at Wurdeja and when I was visiting I'd be able to do a bus run in my school ute early in the morning to pick them up, or parents could drive them if they had working vehicles in the camp.

So, in May 1990, on my 30th birthday, I drove the ninety seven kilometers to Wurdeja in great excitement, ready to impart pearls of knowledge to eager children. I had bought half a dozen loaves of bread in Maningrida and even shot a wallaby on the way and tied it to the truck's bull bar for transport. What better way to arrive than with school lunch?

The ute I drove was a bright yellow Land Cruiser utility truck and I always chose it in preference to the troop carriers which were also a part of the school's fleet. Over the months I customized it by bolting large storage boxes in the tray for my school supplies and installed a gun rack on the back window. I used to travel with a shotgun and a rifle. Hunting was a regular afternoon activity and even on the drive out I could shoot some bush tucker for lunch. I figured I was probably the best armed teacher in Australia.

When we used the truck for school excursions or afternoon trips people would climb aboard and sit on the floor of the tray or on the storage box. It was amazing how many people could get into it. One day we drove to Ramingining, about an hour away, for some shopping and everybody in the community came - I counted thirty six people of all ages crammed into the tray and on the front seat. With all the grocery shopping, the trip home was especially cramped.

On the day Wurdeja School was to open I cheerily turned left at the Debil-debil Tree, bid the devil adieu, apologized for not leaving jambaku and took the track into the community. It had taken three hours to drive from Maningrida and when I got there… nobody. Except for a few dogs the outstation was deserted. I was all dressed up with nowhere to go.

I noticed some tyre tracks heading towards Damdam so I thought I'd go have a look there. Damdam was deserted also but the tracks went on. I followed them for half an hour through the forest and skirted the edge of the grass lands. In the distance smoke told of bush fires. I eventually came across an extensive camp in the bush. All the outstation families from Ji-marda, Ji-malawa, Yilan, Damdam and Wurdeja, and a few others, had come together to burn the grasslands south of Ji-marda for their annual goanna hunt. They were after the sand goanna (*Varanas gouldii*) which was a very favoured tucker indeed. The men torched the grasslands according to a traditional pattern and as the giant lizards fled the flames they were easy to chase down and club. There were a dozen fresh goannas, some well over a meter long, ready to cook, and bits and pieces of leftovers showed that people had already dined well. I was given half a tail for lunch. The tail is 'old lady's' food because it is so easy to eat, but it suited me. Delicious white meat peeled off the bone. It tasted, dare I say it, like chicken.

At the end of May the weather in Arnhem Land must be some of the most pleasant in the world. The warm afternoon sun shed dappled light on the forest floor as I set up my black board. Linda was there with maybe a dozen kids, and we had a school session that afternoon in the shade of the trees on the edge of burning grasslands, with great plumes of smoke heading skyward. The heat created thermals upon which circled fork tailed kites and whistling kites looking for escapees from the flames to feed upon. They would dive bomb small lizards and rodents and then fly quickly away to feed. The "yoooooo...yoo yooo yooo yoo yoo.... yoooooo" whistle, of the whistling kite, the far off screeching of red tailed black cockatoos and the crackle of grass fires was a pleasing background sound to the first day of a school.

It was a reminder of how nomadic these people could be – the first day of Wurdeja School took place a half hour drive away from the community in a temporary bush camp with the attending children having bellies full of fresh goanna meat. To the chagrin of all what was normally an annual hunt didn't happen for a few years after that, because some idiot with a box of matches had lit a fire too early and the entire plain had gone up in smoke before people were ready to hunt. I remember Tommy Steele being particularly annoyed at missing it one year, blaming a "young fella' from Ji-malawa" for the early fire.

Wurdeja quickly became my favourite of all the homeland centers. The mosquitoes were bearable, there was a windmill which pumped plenty of fresh water and I became closer with the families there than the other places I worked. As a result I used to base myself there most of the week and drive to the other schools for the day. I'd then return to Wurdeja and run what we called *homework* – night sessions of school with the kids.

In the beginning I camped under a small tamarind tree on the edge of the community. There were two tin shed houses, an elevated water tank and a few corrugated iron humpies, but all the other 'housing', used by everyone for sleeping regardless of whether they had a house or not, was in the form of stick sleeping platforms. These were about 150 cm off the ground – too high for dogs to jump into, and they were made of sticks tied to forked posts buried in the ground and roofed either with tin or with large sheets of stringy bark. The stick platform was springy, and surprisingly comfortable. Stringybark sheets work well as insulation, so these platforms were also used for sleeping in the heat of the day. Among the platforms were cooking fires with other fires which were for sitting around, always with large billy cans of tea on them.

Wurdeja was the home of one of the most well known of the artists from Arnhem Land, Johnny Bulanbulan, and his wife Laurie Ma-Arbudue. Another artist named Tommy Steele was the senior man and his wife, Rhoda Marburrag, and their kids lived there permanently. Also a number of more transient families stayed for up to months at a time, particularly over the dry season. Tommy's mother, Margaret, was still alive, probably well into her eighties or nineties by then, and she used to sit quietly in the shade each day on a plastic chair and observe everything that went on around her. She had poise and dignity and was held in great respect by everyone. She and I were 'right skin' for marriage and we used to tease and flirt with each other, which everyone found hilarious.

The teachers, Linda Carter and Georgina Mason, were Tommy's daughters. Linda was married and had a small child and when we started the school I was really happy to work with her because she had high literacy and seemed to understand how we could develop the school. Unfortunately she worked with me for only a short time before moving to Ramingining because she had family responsibilities.

Georgina seamlessly took over the school. She was a natural teacher who was in her early twenties, bright, confident and single, and a die-hard Rod

Stewart fan. Her single status worried some of the men around the place, because as I was also single they saw me initially as a bit of a threat. She was 'right skin' for me like her grandmother, so a potential wife. Time healed these worries and Georgina was the main stay of Wurdeja School for the four years I worked there and longer. She was able to do this even though she was almost totally illiterate. She had never been to school and couldn't even write her name correctly, but through the force of her personality she'd get the kids up in the morning, feed them and start school most days whether I was there visiting or not. She was a dynamo who, tragically, was killed recently in a car accident. Her community, and the world, is the poorer without her.

Sometime during my first few days at Wurdeja, Laurie announced,

"That boy Esau, *Ngarrich*, there, he will be your 'special friend'."

Esau Pascoe was a boy of ten, curly haired and mischievous, with the broadest of ready grins. I hardly knew these people at the time so suddenly I was nervous. What did 'special friend' mean? I was a single male of thirty years visiting a remote community who had been given a ten year old boy as a 'special friend'!

"Um, what is that?" I asked carefully.

"He can light your fire, make tea, help you."

This was the community's way of extending hospitality, and indeed Esau became a great friend for years. He was Georgina Mason's half brother, and he had another sister, Fiona and three brothers, Nicky, Joel and Rowan Pascoe. His bush name, Bandidiborta, was a masterpiece of alliteration and a blend of sounds that I used to say because it rolled off the tongue like poetry. Many Aboriginal people retain the old customs of kin relationships and there are certain groups who are not allowed to hear their names, look them in the eye or even sit in the same room. I quickly learned not to use Esau's name in front of his sisters, and in the end I dropped using anyone's bush name because it was hard for me to really sort out who was or wasn't allowed to hear them. The best way to avoid offending people was by using their Balanda names or kin relationship terms.

Esau, at ten, managed to change the entire community's tea drinking habits on my behalf. In the morning someone would make a giant billy of tea by throwing half a dozen teabags into a small amount of water, loading in heaps of sugar and boiling them for several minutes. They would then top the billy up with cold water and leave it on the edge of the fire. There would nearly always be tea ready to drink for anyone with a cup.

My problem was that the tea was too sweet. Esau noticed that I would always make my own billy of tea without sugar and he convinced everyone to leave the sugar out of the billy when I was there so I could share it too. They learned to add sugar to taste afterwards.

Esau and his friends would often cook what I discovered to be a favourite food across the region. It was called *buburu* (a 'contact word' meaning porridge, from the Malay word *bubur*). They would throw a handful of flour into boiling water and make instant flour porridge which then could be sweetened with golden syrup or honey or made into a more substantial meal by adding a tin of bully beef. Sweet *buburu* was a nice treat, but the smell of the tinned bully beef would make me walk a mile!

Another meaning of Esau being a 'special friend' arose later. I'd been visiting for a year and the July school holidays were approaching. We were all sitting round the fire one evening when Laurie told me that everyone had discussed it and I was to take Esau with me on holiday.

I 'ummed' and 'ahhed', and politely refused, but on the drive home the next day I thought, "why not?" After the hospitality and friendship shown me over the previous year I was feeling mean. My holiday plans were merely to visit Darwin and house-sit a friend's place; Esau wouldn't be a problem. I began to plan how I could do it and thought if Esau would come with a friend then it would just be like a school excursion and I could show the two boys the big city.

It was all planned and agreed the next week. Esau and Quincy (Esau's friend and a neighbour of mine in Maningrida) would join me for a week. We'd drive to Darwin, I'd show them around, and they'd fly back to Maningrida.

In the end Quincy couldn't come, but we stayed in Darwin with another teacher who had her own ten year old so it all worked out well. It was a fun week. Esau had never been out of Arnhem Land before, and in fact had rarely even been to the tiny town of Maningrida. We left after school finished.

The road west from Maningrida was a dirt track through thick woollybutt and stringybark forests, across black soil floodplains with numerous river crossings as deep as the Land Cruiser's wind screen, still flowing from the last wet season's run off.

We stopped to eat and had a swim at a creek crossing called *Lady Dreaming.* It took seven or eight hours driving to get to the sealed road at Jabiru so it was well after dark when we got to the South Alligator Motor Inn to buy fuel. Esau was amazed at the lights:

"Wow, is this Darwin?" he asked.

"Not yet," I said, "Just you wait!" His excitement was palpable.

But he was asleep when we arrived at the house in Rapid Creek and I carried him inside, so he saw nothing of Darwin until the next morning when he was woken by the bearded face of our host's gentle giant Irish wolfhound, George. He'd never seen a dog as big as this before and was agog.

We went straight to Casuarina Mall. Esau had $400 to spend on presents for his family and this was what he wanted to do first. The mall was enormous; he'd never been in a building bigger than Maningrida Clinic! Everything was new to him. At one point he stopped and looked at the mannequins in a store window and nearly fell about laughing. Naked store dummies are really funny I guess, I just hadn't noticed before.

Esau bought a football and clothes and toys for his family and himself. When we left the mall we were both heavily laden and he was dressed in a lime green basketball jacket with a baseball cap placed backwards on his head, looking like he'd just come out of Harlem. We spent the rest of the week doing tourist things around Darwin – a Jumping Crocodile Tour, the wildlife park, the museum - but in hind sight I think he was ready to go back the first day as he already had so much to tell his brothers, and presents to take them.

The first few months of Wurdeja School passed quickly, with all lessons taking place on the school's blue tarp, but the looming wet season brought about some changes.

One day I turned up as normal, ready to camp under the tamarind tree again, but Tommy had had other ideas. Whilst I had been away they'd built me my own stick shelter – an extra strong platform upon which my swag and Turkey would fit very comfortably. During heavy rainstorms it was as dry and cozy as anyone would ever need. The only trouble was, for a privacy seeking Balanda such as me, it was right plum in the middle of all the other sleeping platforms. I slept in it for several weeks, amid all the noises of the night that thirty people can make, with dogs fighting underneath. I felt really welcome but longed for the privacy and quiet of the bush. One night a man named Wayne had a fit on the ground under my platform. He fitted occasionally and they were extremely noisy affairs that lasted ten or twenty minutes but everyone else just ignored him, so that's what I tried to do as well.

With the approaching wet season we also needed to build a shelter for the school. One day after school we had gone crabbing at a place called Gumugumuk. There was a small beach here among large areas of mangrove. On the beach we found two large panels of what I took to be a ship's freezer because they clearly were insulating panels of sorts that fitted together with a tongue and groove mechanism. They had floated in on the tide. Each was about three meters long by one and a half meters wide. We salvaged them and tied them to the canopy of the Land Cruiser and took them back to Wurdeja that afternoon.

The next week I called in at Maningrida's rubbish tip, which was in the bush a couple a kilometers outside of town. Here I picked up ten or so sheets of corrugated iron and, along with a bag of roofing nails and strapping from the store, I returned to Wurdeja. With the help of the kids and Jimmy Mason from Damdam we cut down forked trees for posts and long staffs as rafters. We used the freezer panels as one of the walls and long sheets of corrugated iron as a second wall. Then we roofed it with more corrugated iron and hung a shade tarpaulin on one of the open sides.

I painted one of the panels with blackboard paint and we found a large picnic style table at Ji-marda that they let us borrow. I asked the school to purchase a large metal cupboard, a radio and a solar panel with a car battery to run the radio. The cupboard became a waterproof and dog proof storage area for school equipment and the radio room all in one. The Wurdeja School kids joined the other outstation schools in the daily reading program to a teacher on listening duty in Maningrida. Early on we extended the roofed area with a blue tarp, but found more tin eventually, so it was quite a construction. That this was the basis of a Government school building for the next two and a half years in modern day Australia seems unlikely, but that's how it was for a number of outstation schools.

With the new 'building', I could also politely now use the school as an alternative sleeping place to my stick platform. To the amazement of the kids I braved the spirits and ghosts in the bush and slept alone, away from the safety of the group. The school was built right on the edge of the clearing near the trees which the old people said were full of spirits and should be avoided. I asked Rhoda one night if she believed in the stories she would tell the kids about the spirits.

"Nah," she said. "We just tell the kids that so they won't go walking about at night. Big mob of snakes there."

Wurdeja was an excellent place for me to stay. It was central to the five outstation schools I was eventually running in the area and there was so much to do after school. Our charter as homeland centre teachers was to run school for four hours each day then just be there using English and interacting with the community. Timing was amazingly flexible. In the hot season we could start school at 6 am and be finished by 10 am, but in the cold we'd start much later. I'd be camping in the community with a vehicle and a sense of adventure and after school time I figured anything I did with kids was valuable in educational terms because we'd be speaking English and sharing experiences. We'd go hunting or fishing most days, I'd take 'story' videos of the kids' activities, and photographs which I turned into dozens of photo books the kids would read around cooking fires wherever we happened to be.

I always did a 'bus trip' to Ji-malawa and Damdam outstations before school. Dalma, a lady from Ji-malawa, started rounding the kids up in the morning and they'd be ready by the time I arrived to jump in the truck and come back to the school. Dalma eventually became the first teacher at Ji-malawa School, which we opened a few years later. One of my favourite places in the forest was on the Ji-malawa road. There was a thick stand of *Livistonia* sand palms and tall cycads. These were the biggest of the slow growing cycad palms I ever saw and they must have been hundreds of years old. I used to ensure I was alone during the bus run so I could stop there for a few minutes in peace for my morning constitutional.

Wurdeja School ran for three years before it 'proved' itself as a viable school to the Government. The families who lived here were sufficiently stable for the Government to spend money and to build a proper building here. This seems harsh, but there are numerous school buildings funded at enormous expense across Arnhem Land in areas where people don't live any more. Chris Baldwin, by then Principal in Maningrida, gave me the task of designing a school in consultation with Georgina, Tommy and the rest of the Wurdeja community.

What they wanted was simple. The bush construction we had made three years before had served well. They wanted a school building the same design, only bigger. So we designed a building with two solid and two open walls, which we improved by installing four large roller doors which faced the community, so the school was always open and welcoming. It was slightly elevated with a wide veranda right around it, and had a store room and a battery room for the solar power system. At the back it had a teacher's accommodation room with toilet and shower. I initially balked at adding in the toilet and shower. I thought it would be odd and unfair for me to have the only bathroom in Wurdeja. Chris insisted, rightly, that we put it in because over time the community would be developed, but we'd never get the funding to add in a bathroom later.

Life changed with the addition of the new school, and solar electricity. With lights we had 'night school' often, because that was what the kids asked for. I could also have a hot shower at the end of the day, and sleep under a fan. Unfortunately the batteries were always flattened by long electric cables running to video players and TVs in the community. People would sit up all night watching Jacky Chan movies.

The school was officially opened, amid much merriment and welcoming dancers, by Maurice Rioli. It was his first official engagement as a newly elected Member of the Northern Territory Legislative Council and was described in his maiden speech to Parliament.

I was promoted the next year to a town based job in Maningrida although I still managed a few weekend trips back to Wurdeja, particularly during the prawn season, or to watch initiation ceremonies of ex students. Another visiting teacher moved in and the new school building, which was still a novelty to me, became the norm for her.

4

WULAKI

Gamardi people were always closely associated with the Burarra people of Wurdeja and the other homeland centers on that side of the Blyth River. This was mainly through friendships and intermarriage between the tribes because they were Wulaki rather than Burarra and they spoke a Yolngu language named Djinang, more associated with language groups in Eastern Arnhem Land than the west.

Before the new straight road was pushed though the bush in about 1993 the track to the coast at Ji-marda used to meander through the bush. It actually went through the dwellings in the Gamardi community, so every time I visited Ji-marda, Yilan, or Wurdeja by road I'd pass right through their back yards. The community had a single mud brick house with wide verandas and a small collection of tin shacks, a windmill and a raised water tank. There was a cleared strip of land running several hundred meters down to the Blyth River and someone had built a little landing out of bush timber on the bank. The coffee

Garmardi School 1992. The teacher is Kathleen Barrgitjbar.

brown river was about a hundred meters wide here and it moved swiftly in and out with the tides. The *tucker boat* would come up river to bring food and goods during the wet season when the roads were impassable and the tucker man, Peter Toms, would use the landing to display his wares.

There were always numerous kids running around the community and one day out of curiosity I stopped to say *g'day* to the people there.

The community leaders were Terry Ganadila and a couple both in their early forties, Michael *Young Michael* Gajawula and Margaret Rinbuma. Michael and Margaret had several children and grand children in their camp. Margaret was a proper bushie and she said she hadn't been to Maningrida or Ramingining in nearly ten years, and she stayed at Gamardi nearly all the time.

There was an elder living there also named Michael who was a renowned wood carver. He was clearly elderly with snow white hair and he quickly became known to me as *Old Michael* and I always called Margaret's Michael *Young Michael*.

Young Michael and Margaret were glad I had stopped.

"Maybe you put school here too?" asked Michael. "Big mob of kids here!"

We did a head count. There were at least a dozen school aged children, and several three year olds. A woman named Kathleen Barrgitjbar said she wanted to be a teacher and had worked for a while in education when she was single. Kathleen had an eight year old daughter named Nina Jinmatata, whom I recognized as she had been in my first class at Maningrida. In fact I recognized a number of the other kids too – Eric Pascoe, Katrina, Theresa and Simon, as itinerant Maningrida visitors.

Kathleen was a very intelligent woman, quite well educated and married to an excellent bushman named Johnny Watjpurali.

"Long time ago we had a school in Gamardi, but it's finished now. We got a building there, that old shop," said Michael as he pointed to a tin shed.

We walked over to a strangely tall corrugated iron building that at one time had been a shop or store room of some kind. It had locked double wooden doors on the front and four tightly closed louvered windows and when we opened the door

I was hit by a heat wave. It had been used to store some items which were private or for ceremonies, and it was kept closed and locked. In the sun, any unlined construction made of corrugated iron is like an oven inside in the tropics and this building was proof of that. Inside, on each side of the entrance were wooden platforms about 40 centimeters high with a ground level space between them. Despite the furnace-like interior I thought the building had good possibilities. The two separate platforms would make an easy division between the younger kids and the older kids so we could have a primary and a secondary section.

"OK, Michael, I'll go and talk to *Johnrattigan*, see what he reckons."

John, as usual, was supportive so I started to make plans to convert the building into a school. There were about a dozen old desks and chairs in a school storeroom in Maningrida and I immediately appropriated them. I also found a new blackboard and a cupboard which I took without asking, on the grounds that it's sometimes better to ask forgiveness than permission. The only extra cost would be the installation of a school radio.

My major concern was the heat of the building, but I thought that when it became too hot we could easily take the kids outside and sit in the shade on a tarpaulin.

And so, on Tuesday 2nd April 1991, Gamardi School officially opened its doors and became the tenth outstation school serviced by Maningrida Community Education Center. We began teaching with 13 students. Kathleen quickly proved an excellent teacher and ran the school well and some weeks it attracted more than 20 students. Gamardi was associated both with people from Ramingining in the east and Maningrida in the west and it was about equidistant from them so visitors would come from either community and would stay several weeks or months. As a result the school numbers fluctuated quite a bit.

I liked Gamardi very much and spent a lot of time there. I went to the Maningrida tip one afternoon and discovered a pile of fiber board sheeting, then spent a weekend installing them as inside walls of the school to provide insulation. It made the shed a little more comfortable in the heat.

I also built myself a house. I was inspired by Murray Garde who had built himself one at Yikarrakkal, with cypress pine beams and concrete floors. His house was open and breezy and cool. Mick Kubaku, the community leader and a renowned artist had painted some *Mimih* spirits in the rock wall inside the house and it was a delightful place to stay. I had spent several weekends helping Murray and the teenage young men of Yikarrakkal building it. We cut down cypress pines and used the school ute to take the logs back to the community and brought in some second hand tin for the roof. Yikarrakkal is well into the Stone Country so rocks were easy to find.

My own house was a much simpler design. I returned to the Maningrida tip one day and there was a pile of plywood floor sheets taken up from a renovation of the nurses' quarters. I took the lot, and some tin, and bought some nails and aluminium strapping. With a few bush timber posts Old Michael and I cut from the forest the house took about a day to build. It had an elevated floor sitting on some leftover mud bricks, a built in desk, one solid wall on the side the rain usually came in from, and two walls that could open up with shutters. The fourth wall was just an open space, looking out into the forest. I used a floor panel and some mud bricks to make a raised bed, upon which I could unroll my swag. Permanent hooks in strategic places allowed me to hang my mosquito net and my kerosene lantern. The house was in the shade of a small *Melina* tree and cool during the day. I was very proud of it and have good memories of using it as a study – many of my essays for my masters degree were written at the desk by the light of the kerosene lamp, on a laptop computer plugged into the school ute.

One other thing I picked up at the tip proved very popular - an old bath. I installed it under the windmill where there was always dripping water and it became a great place for the kids to play on a hot day. Old bath tubs were occasionally dumped at the Maningrida tip, so I salvaged any I could find and ended up taking them out to Wurdeja and Ji-marda also.

Often the Gamardi school building was just too hot to work in, so we'd be outside on the tarp. But one day in October, as sweat dripped from my forehead onto a child's school work, I had had enough.

"Right!" I said emphatically. "Let's get out of here. Time for school somewhere cooler. Let's go to Nemerilli Crossing and have school there."

A big cheer greeted this news. Nemerilli Crossing was where the main road, which was forged through to Ramingining from Maningrida in 1964, crossed the Blyth River. The road actually hit the river a couple of kilometers away, but then turned sharply upstream to reach Nemerilli. When it was being built the road makers had no real plan to cross at this point but a local elder had told them how easy it would be and that a bridge wasn't needed. So when they arrived at the river a couple of kilometers north, they just turned right and pushed the road south until they reached Nemerilli and the crossing there has been used ever since and new comers wonder at the strange right hand turn in the road. The river at Nemerilli is a series of sandstone rock ledges with cool swimming holes in the shade of giant *Melaleuca* trees. We could be pretty sure there were no crocodiles lurking there as we could see the bottom of the river through the shallow, crystal clear water. It meant loading all the kids into the ute and a 28 kilometer drive, but we had school for the day on the cool riverbank, including some book work on a tarp by the water and some English speaking and singing practice actually sitting in the water. We cooked damper and a cat fish one of the older boys caught in the fire and stayed there until early evening. After that day, in October and November when the heat became really oppressive, we'd regularly move the school to the river.

One day we were at our customary 'dinner camp' a little downstream from the crossing when the adults started hushing the kids.

"Shh, shhh, quiet."

Everyone listen intently.

"What is it, Johnny?" I asked.

"It's a dragon," he replied. "It's in the river up at the crossing."

That was the first I'd heard of dragons, or people believing in them, in the region. I could feel the tension in the air. The kids were quiet for the first time that day and their eyes rolled with trepidation.

"How do you know?" I asked.

"Look," said Johnny. "In the river: see his saliva?"

It was true. Flowing in the river's current were strings of frothy bubbles. I'd never seen them before, and they certainly looked like saliva. It was peculiar, but over the next half hour or so the tension eased and everyone started to relax and the day went on as normal. The dragon must have moved on.

The funny thing was we went back to that spot many times and the dragon's frothy 'saliva' was always in the river, but no one ever mentioned the dragon again. I think I was conned.

Someone in the 1980s had discovered that outstation children were entitled to receive a Government allowance called Assistance for Isolated Children, known as AIC money, and Maningrida teachers had met with homeland centre leaders and discussed this with them. It was 'school money' their kids, or at least their families, would get if they attended school in outstations, (although students of Maningrida hub school weren't eligible) and the teachers at the time made a deal with the community leaders. They would do the administration and accounting for 'school money' if the homelands people were happy to allow half of it to be spent on the schools. Everyone seemed happy with this arrangement and by the time I arrived in Maningrida the AIC money that was the school's share was quite substantial. It had already bought a Land Cruiser "troop carrier" and the school boat, paid for school excursions, sports carnivals, electronic equipment, and a whole range of other things. It was a real boon to the schools. The parents' half was distributed to the families at the end of each term.

The administration was simple. The teachers would fill in forms, photocopy them, and then take them to the outstation to be signed by the parents.

For me in the first year of Gamardi School it was also a useful way of finding out who was related to whom. Margaret Rinbuma looked after several children, one of which was a grandchild, and she signed the form quite happily.

"Sign here please." I said.

"What? Put a cross?" She asked.

"Ok, no problem." Margaret wouldn't have been the first person to sign her name with a cross on an AIC form.

The next year, things went a little differently.

"Sign here," I said, proffering the form.

She took the pen, and with a flourish signed her name in beautiful old fashioned script: *Margaret Rinbuma*.

"Hang on a minute, *Mununa*," I said. "Last year you signed with a cross."

Margaret looked at me.

"Yes," she said, "You asked me to."

It turned out Margaret had been to school at Milingimbi Mission in the 1950s for many years and was relatively highly educated.

Apart from the river, most of the country for tens of kilometers in all directions from Gamardi is a forested plain. One peculiarity was a circular sinkhole, not far to the west and just off the road. The hole was perhaps 15 meters deep with a diameter of about 20 meters. I used to stop there occasionally just to look at it and wonder at its formation – most of the rocks in the area were minerals like bauxite and I had always associated sinkholes with limestone so I found it odd. Michael had an easy explanation for it. He explained that it was an important *Dreaming site* and in the Dreamtime one of the ancestral beings, a giant tortoise, had come out of the ground here. It had then travelled north to a place near Ji-malawa where it had made a small billabong in the forest where it could live more happily. I knew the billabong well and had been there with Ji-malawa people hunting for tortoises, which live there in large numbers. It was a small depression in otherwise flat ground without any connection to a creek or a river. Michael's traditional explanation provided a reason for its existence that all the local people were happy with.

5
ART AND ARTISTS

The Maningrida Arts and Culture Centre has long had very high standards for the art they accept from the artists they support. This has resulted, arguably, in the highest quality Indigenous art in Australia and some of the most well known Aboriginal artists live in the remote homeland centers where we ran schools. In the 1990s artists such as England Bangala, Mick Kubaku, James Iyuna, Lena Yarinkurra, Johnny Bulanbulan and others would create their art right next to where we'd be teaching.

Johnny Bulanbulan lived at Wurdeja. He was a very famous man and was a brilliant artist who had travelled the world to his exhibitions. When I first met him he'd just won a court case that has become a land mark case for artists' rights, written about by undergraduate students ever since. He had sued a manufacturer who had 'stolen' one of his painting designs, *Magpie Geese and Water Lilies at the Waterhole*, and was selling it as a printed design on T-shirts. Johnny had won the case, stopping the production,

Johnny Bulanbulan was commissioned to make these bark canoes by a museum. He made them in the bush a few hundred meters from Wurdeja School.

and was awarded $15,000 in damages. His point though, was not that they were using his work without permission or payment, it was that the images were 'title to his land' and no one else had the right to use them. They weren't ever for sale to be reproduced by anyone else. *Magpie Geese and Water Lilies at the Waterhole* is a magnificent painting. It shows a dozen magpie geese with black, brown or yellow necks heading to one of three waterholes. In one of the waterholes is curled the head end of a large snake, and a couple of long necked tortoises move among the geese and their nests, filled with eggs. It still rests in the collection of the Northern Territory Museum of Arts and Sciences.

Bulanbulan's problem wasn't new. Another artist whose work was famously used without his permission was David Malangi from Eastern Arnhem Land. Malangi's painting was used on the Australian one dollar note in 1966 and the row that followed ended up with him getting a $1,000 payment for his work, which he was pretty happy with at the time. You can imagine his surprise when he first went to the shop and received the new $1 note in his change.

Bulanbulan was a Ganalbingu man who came from country further east than Wurdeja, but he lived there with Laurie and his family for many years. I knew he spoke Ganalbingu, Burarra, Djinang and some of the Gupupunyu languages and one day we worked out he could speak seven different languages, including English. When a truck arrived in the community one afternoon and a man spoke to him in a language I didn't recognize I asked him what it was. He mentioned a language I'd never heard of before.

"But you didn't tell me that. Is that another language you can speak?" I asked.

"No," he said, "But I can *listen* to that one."

I never found out how many he could 'listen' to, but it made me feel an intellectual minnow in my feeble attempts to learn Burarra, or any other language for that matter.

He never ceased to amaze me with language. One day we were chatting and a tractor drove through the community. Not a single word could be heard above the noise of the machine but Johnny waved at the driver, who waved back and drove on.

"What's happening, Johnny, where's he going?" I asked, not expecting him to know anything more than I.

"Ahh, that Jacky Kurrumulu he's bogged near Nemerilli and Jamesy's going to Ji-malawa for a chain. Pull him out."

"How the hell do you know that?" I was astonished.

"He told me," said Johnny waving his hand incomprehensibly in front of me.

Sign language was mostly a mystery to me, although I did kind of get a feeling for it over the years. Murray Garde, a sponge of all things 'language', was, of course also fluent in *Bininj* sign language. There was one time he got into a bit of a problem:

> Having lived on outstations for so many years I not only learned to speak *Kunwinjku* but I had also internalized the local Aboriginal sign language, which we all used on a daily basis on the outstations where I was living. On that occasion I was at the (four-way) intersection in down town Maningrida and was waiting for someone else to come to my vehicle. The local police officer arrived (on the roadside opposite me) and waited for me to move.
>
> I indicated by local sign language that I would stay where I was and that he should pass me, a signal involving a closed fist and one or two up and down movements of the wrist: "I'm staying here."
>
> I should have realized of course that this signal wouldn't work cross-culturally and that only when I saw the police officer drive up to my window and start abusing me did I realize that this local signal had no currency with the constabulary.
>
> He protested I was being offensive and in between the yelling I attempted to somehow explain the intricacies of *Bininj* sign language. I realized it was a lost cause.

One week I introduced Johnny Bulanbulan to a Melbourne based Chinese artist named Joe Xiao Ping. Joe tagged along for the week whilst I was teaching and spent a lot of time with Johnny and other artists, drawing them with charcoal and sharing art. It started a relationship that lasted until Johnny's death a few years ago. It was truly inspirational in terms of art but also in cross cultural friendship – even ABC Television got in on the act and produced a one hour special about the two of them.

Joe camped with me and protected his art supplies vigilantly. I wondered why he worked so hard to care for them.

"Ahh, yes" he said. "Last week I went with Murray to Mumeka, and they had a bloody pig there that ate all my stuff!"

He had lost much of the equipment which he'd specially imported from China so what he had left was particularly precious. He was putting it away carefully one night at Gamardi when he leant over the kerosene hurricane lamp I used and somehow pushed the top of it onto his shoulder. It was very hot and burned him badly and poor Joe spent a painful night, but in the morning even he had to laugh about it – burned on his shoulder from the top of the lamp, like some patriotic tattoo in backwards letters were the words,

"MADE IN CHINA"

The Burarra art scene was one of many across the Top End of Australia, but there were distinctive differences in the style and presentation of the art. Maningrida painters were encouraged by the Arts and Crafts Centre, in those days managed by Dianne Moon, to paint purely on bark sheets. Some wanted art paper for its ease in transport and preparation, as Gunbalanya Art Centre had introduced for its Kunwinjku artists and as a result some of the Eastern Kunwinjku people had moved to Gunbalanya to take advantage of it. Dianne and her committee of senior artists were adamant that they could be a supplier of artists' supplies, but Maningrida artists would paint mainly on bark.

"You're keeping them in the Bark Ages," I exclaimed one day when I had carefully delivered someone's giant bark painting from the bush in my school truck. But no one else thought this comment was particularly useful, so I let it slide.

Burarra paintings, like most from Arnhem Land, are distinguished by fine cross hatchings of parallel lines called *rraak*. Almost all use the same earth colours of different ochres and charcoal – brown, black, yellow and white. Burarra paintings differ from other groups in Central Arnhem Land and many Burarra artists seem to fill every square centimeter of the background with rraak and commonly paint the figures in a single colour. The Kunwinjku and Rembarrnga artists often paint an animal, or a plant in isolation on a bark. I have a giant painting of two fresh water crocodiles by Lena Yaringula, a lady from Borlkdjam, which is a fine example of an 'X-ray' style painting. The crocodiles' insides are revealed in detail. They have been hunting and have both been successful. One holds a barramundi in its jaws and the other a small wallaby (*gornabola*). The animals' outlines are in white lines, but the background is plain brown.

I have some paintings that tell stories that involve a large number of animals. One by Jimmy Pascoe from Ji-malawa shows the nearby billabong, which was the final resting place for the giant tortoise that appears in the story about how the sink hole near Gamardi, about 20 kilometers away, was created. A dozen fat goannas and a large number of snakes and long necked tortoises are heading there and yam vines wind across the landscape.

Many ancestral stories appear in the paintings of the region. One common story concerned the Wawilak sisters, who are the ancestors of the Dhuwa moiety. The sisters had come overland from the east, naming birds, animals and plants as they travelled. They had many adventures which appear in song cycles and dances in a number of ceremonies across Arnhem Land. The sisters were killed in the end by Ngalyod, the Rainbow Serpent, because the older sister had 'polluted' a waterhole with her menstrual blood. The serpent was so angry he created a great storm and ate both sisters and the younger sister's new born baby.

Artists being artists, of course, means that any rules of style can be easily broken. I have a great bark painting by Reggie Wood from Gochan Jiny-Jirra which just shows a bunch of animals in a cartoon style pose. There's little that is traditional about this one.

The tribes that come from the Stone Country such as the Gagadju, Rembarrnga and Kunwinjku have always had ready places to paint permanent reminders of their existence - the rocks themselves. In the escarpment south of Maningrida and spread across the Top End are rock paintings that are 20,000 or more years old. Some exist in galleries a hundred meters long whilst others are single paintings on small overhangs.

Big Bill Neiji, from Canon Hill, took me to some remarkable galleries when I worked as a ranger at the East Alligator. Big Bill was a much respected elder and traditional owner of much of the country that became the northern part of Kakadu National Park. My introduction to rock art was a gallery at a place where "the cockatoo split the rock." We called it *Nadaj* and the gallery wraps around an escarpment not far from the major road through the National Park. It's a site the owners have never opened to the public and it was a privilege to see it. Big Bill explained that it wasn't his country, he came from Canon Hill, but he wanted me to have a look anyway.

It was November and the 'build up' season before the wet arrived - hot and humid with little rain. Bill led me through a scrubby forest of acacia trees and young spear grass towards the escarpment. There were only about three hundred meters to walk, but when we arrived at the small stream at the base of the cliffs I was already drenched in sweat. We paused to leap into a small pool to cool off. Well, I leapt. Bill, a dignified elder, slowly eased himself in the crystal clear water.

"Where do we go now, Bill?"

"Little way up there," he pointed. Bill had the deepest voice I can remember and its timbre seemed to reverberate like distant thunder among the rocks.

So we climbed. It wasn't far, perhaps double the height of the forest and when we skirted around a boulder on a ledge I caught my breath - ahead were hundreds of paintings on the walls and roof of a long overhang. There were crocodiles and barramundi, birds of every description, wallabies and antelopine kangaroos and hundreds of hand prints. A long rainbow serpent stretched across the ceiling. There were 'X-ray' style paintings overlaying older red ochre paintings. Some of the red ochre paintings were so old they were barely visible.

The overhang was cool, naturally air conditioned with extraordinary views across the forest to Canon Hill in the west and we spent more than an hour there relaxing among some extraordinary paintings. I have been in great galleries from the Louvre to the Prada, but this little gallery of Nadaj, one of many hundreds of similar galleries spread across Arnhem Land, rates right up there with them.

The Arnhem Land galleries record history too. The climate has changed over the last 20,000 years. Wetlands have come and gone, species of plants and animals have changed and people kept painting through it all. For example, clearly visible only from a boat on an overhang above the East Alligator River, there's a single painting of an animal which is clearly a *thylacine*, or Tasmanian tiger, which has been extinct on the Australian mainland for thousands of years. There are at least another 13 other distinct *thylacine* paintings known so they must have been a fairly conspicuous member of the local fauna. When dogs arrived in Australia, possibly as pets with families who migrated across from Asia, their arrival was the beginning of the end for the *thylacine* and other species on the mainland. The dog that became the Australian dingo never made it to Tasmania, so some of the original wildlife of the country managed to survive there quite well, at least until European settlement. At Lake Nitchie in New South Wales archeologists discovered a necklace of 170 Tasmanian devil teeth, in the grave of a man who lived more than 6,000 years ago.

Many rock paintings are more modern and are called 'contact paintings'. Bill showed me paintings at Canon Hill of ocean going boats called *prahus* whose Maccassan sailors used to collect the sea slugs known as trepang, or *beche de mare*, that they could pick up in the shallows and boil in giant vats, then salt to preserve them on the beaches. There were pictures of white men smoking pipes and carrying rifles - perhaps the legendary buffalo hunter Paddy Cahill himself in a portrait.

I quickly discovered that most people were artists to some extent. Some were more skilled than others in the painting of the rraak, so became more marketable in the art centers, but everyone could and would produce something if the desire was there. Once we did a bark painting project at Wurdeja

School. All the kids painted their own pieces of bark and I am pretty sure that at some stage or other every adult in the community came over to help the kids on their masterpieces. I was given one of them to keep by Esau and it is suspiciously like the paintings that Tommy Steele used to do. In this way the young learn from the old, I guess.

The bark comes directly from the forest, of course, but cutting it is only really possible in the wet season. It needs several months to cure properly so that it remains flat and suitable for an artwork. I went with Young Michael from Gamardi on a bark collecting expedition one wet season afternoon. We simply walked into the forest until he found a large healthy stringybark eucalyptus tree.

"This one is good," he said, taking out his small axe.

He quickly cut through the bark in two jagged lines around the tree, followed by a vertical line to join them. He hit the tree along the cuts with the back of his axe head which loosened the bark so he could then push the axe head in behind it and lever to carefully unpeel it from the trunk. The two meter long sheet of wet living bark came free remarkably easily. It rolled itself up and it was easy to shoulder and carry back to Gamardi. We left the once proud bush tree, ring-barked and doomed to the ubiquitous termites and dry rot, to join the legion of other dead trees scattered throughout the forest that had given up their bark for art or shelter.

Once home Michael 'cooked' the bark in the heat of a fire and then flattened it and weighed it down with stones so it would dry straight over the next few weeks. With a couple of sticks sewn across the top and bottom to keep it flat it would then be ready for painting.

Gamardi people live kilometers away from the escarpment so traditionally never painted on rocks. However, stringybark sheets like this one were always used for building shelters against the rain and it was a simple jump for them to become painting boards as well. The oldest bark paintings in existence were collected in 1878 at Port Essington – they are small pictures, one of a goanna and the other an emu or a cassowary. A little later, in 1884, an explorer of the South Alligator River system, Captain Frederick Carrington, discovered some wet season bark shelters which had designs painted on their inside walls. Being bark in a tropical climate these paintings were ephemeral at best, but Carrington managed to sample some and they're now preserved in the South Australian Museum.

During last century the coastal people quickly learned that there was a market for paintings done this way, so artworks, similar to the traditional designs painted on the wet season shelters or the bodies of young initiates, can now be found on walls across the world. It is big business and galleries guard their artists jealously. When the kids from Gamardi School and I went on a field trip to Alice Springs one year I noticed a bark painting in a gallery that was painted in Gamardi. The artist's daughter, Sandra, was with me and I asked the gallery operator if she'd mind if I took a photograph of the work to show her father where it had ended up. The answer was a categorical

"No." Photography of art was impossible, but she did allow me to take a broader picture of the shop with Sandra standing next to the bark painting.

Old Michael in Gamardi was a renowned wood carver. He'd journey out to the bush and cut down the soft wooded kapok trees. These were once wide spread although not very common in the local area and I believe they're now becoming quite rare as more wood carvers seek them out. Their cotton wool-like seed masses were once used to stuff saddles or mattresses. They flower and seed at a time of the year when they have almost no leaves, their large seed pods stark against the sky. Often their trunks and branches are green with chlorophyll, revealing the secret of how they get the energy to grow their seed pods without leaves.

The soft wood of the kapok is easily carved. Old Michael made it even easier by doing the bulk of the cutting with his little chainsaw. His carvings of figures were 'primitive', with little fine detail, but once painted with ochre they developed a charm of their own.

Kunwinjku wood carvers like James Iyuna from Mumeka, who also painted barks and didgeridoos, often carved spirit figures called *Mimih*. Mimih are long thin mischievous spirits which are never seen because as you approach they are thin enough to disappear into the cracks in the rocks. Paintings of mimih more than 20,000 years old have been discovered in the escarpment. They are dynamic figures, often heavily armed with barbed spears and they always seem to be actively doing something. Mimih are common subjects in rock paintings and on barks and are easily carved because of their simply morphology. The wood of these carvings, being light, is readily attacked by insects and if left out doesn't last long. That's OK, apparently, as the artists claim they are made to decay as part of the art.

I always liked the idea of mimih. They were supposed to cause trouble like European goblins or imps and it's apparent that many people really believe they exist. If something was mislaid in a camp people would suggest that maybe a mimih had taken it when backs were turned.

Arnhem Landers are also prolific produces of crafted objects. Common in Central Arnhem Land, for example, are hollow log fish traps. These are laid in a stream with bait in one end, and fork tailed cat fish and other scavenging fish will swim up the log to eat the bait. They are caught by inserting a stick through specially cut holes to block off their escape. A number of artists also paint them with totems like snakes and catfish.

Bone pole coffins are also hollow logs, but with fewer modifications. I bought one once from England Bangala from Gochan Jiny-Jirra which resembles a giant didgeridoo about a meter and a half in length, but with a bore of about 20 centimeters. What makes it a work of art is the extraordinary painting that Bangala chose to decorate it with. Traditionally bone pole coffins were used by relatives of a deceased person in final funeral ceremonies where the bones would be left high in a tree inside the coffin. I saw some ancient coffins in a tree just outside Marrkolidjban once which had been there so long none of the young people knew who they belonged to any more.

Woven art and crafts are also very common. James Iyuna is a renowned weaver of fish traps using skills handed down to him from his father, Anchor Kulumba. These are large conical traps woven from jungle vines which are occasionally still used. Some of the early photographs of the area show people fishing with them quite successfully on the flood plains.

In the middle of the last century new technologies were introduced into Arnhem Land. Early missionaries like Shepherdson encouraged basket weaving as a new economic activity and Tongan and Fijian missionaries at Goulburn Island taught women to make coiled fiber baskets and mats, and people began to experiment with natural dyes to enhance the beauty of their work. In central Arnhem Land the fibers of the sand palm (*Livistonia*), *pandanus* trees or sedges are commonly used to make distinctive baskets and mats which have for many decades now found a ready market in the cities of the world. Maccassan fishermen used to harvest some plants to make natural dyes during their trepang voyages to the coast so the practice wasn't new to Aboriginal people, but the new 'technology' of large kerosene tins or flour drums allowed people to boil water for longer times on their fires. The dyes are natural pigments made from boiling certain barks or crushed roots. Brown colours come from the inner bark of the woollybutt tree and reds from the roots of a smaller plant known as redroot or bloodwort. Other tree barks are used, like green plum tree for a red dye and the red bush apple tree for orange. Greys and blacks can be made by using the ash of burned quinine tree leaves and branches and fruits from sand palms can create purple dyes.

The fibers of *pandanus* leaves are stripped from the long spiky leaves and then boiled for many hours with the dyes. The longer they are boiled the stronger the final colours become.

Basket making is an activity mostly of women and as most of the outstation teachers were women a common activity after school or in the evenings was making baskets. Georgina Mason at Wurdeja used to make baskets with arm handles in the style I imagine Little Red Riding Hood would have used. Melba Gunjarrwanga at Mumeka was an accomplished weaver, not only of baskets but of large spiral floor mats.

People also make rough string from the bark of kurrajongs, smooth string from the roots of banyan trees or very fine string from a vine called *burney* vine. From the string they make a variety of useful items, such as sacred dilly bags, arm ornaments for ceremonies, general use dilly bags, large string bags, fish nets and sieves. The women would always carry string bags they had made on foraging trips and they were incredibly strong and lasted well. One time I estimated Georgina Mason had collected more than 20 kilograms of *an-bombala* mud mussels in her string bag, and as I was press ganged into being the porter back to the dinner camp, I can confirm it was easily sturdy enough to carry them.

Arnhem Landers used to routinely make their

own canoes from a tree trunk or bark. The early Europeans wrote of being greeted by people paddling out to meet them or crossing wide rivers in canoes that had been left on the banks but in the 1990s the only canoes I saw made were made on commission for buyers through the Arts and Crafts Center. Near the school in Maningrida a large log was carved into a four meter canoe by two men with small axes. It was a labour of about two weeks and when it was finished they held sea trials with a triangular woven *pandanus* fiber sail for a film that was being shot in the area, then packed it off to a museum somewhere.

Bark canoes were smaller and more flimsy, but quicker to make with readily available materials. One year Johnny Bulanbulan was commissioned to make two bark canoes at Wurdeja. We were excited for the kids from Wurdeja School to be involved because bark canoe making is fast becoming a lost art, so we visited his makeshift workshop every day to follow the events.

Johnny had cut two very large sheets of stringy-bark, one for each canoe. Using a system of sticks for ribs and hot wire to burn holes he sewed the canoes together at each end and splayed the middle out. A single pole went down the middle of each canoe to provide strength and other poles acted as gunwales along the sides. He collected plant gums from cypress pines and other trees and used it to waterproof the joints, then left them to dry out for a few days under a tarpaulin. At one point he cooked the bark over a small fire so that the canoes dried into their final shape. The completed canoes were amazingly strong. The largest was more than three meters long but they were never used and were also packed up for a museum.

Johnny was, of course, better known for his painting than his canoe making. Somewhere in America there is a giant painting attributed to Bulanbulan, the great master Aboriginal artist. It's probably viewed by hundreds of thousands of people a year, but no one would ever imagine that some of it was painted by a Balanda school teacher sitting in the dust in a remote outstation in Central Arnhem Land. This painting is enormous, perhaps five meters long and two meters wide. It was a $20,000 consignment, unusually for Johnny on canvas, and it was especially commissioned by an American art museum. In a break one day the kids and I wandered over from the school to watch him paint it and he invited us to help with the background. We sat along the edges of the canvas with tins of Johnny's ochre and some small brushes I had brought across from the school. All the kids chipped in and did their bit, but the top right hand corner was all mine, and for a brief moment I felt like an apprentice artist to a master.

6
ANIMALS

Aboriginal people in the bush are well tuned into the environment because they are a part of it every day. One of the results of this is that outstations become the home of many animals found in the wild and brought home as pets. Birds like blue herons, burdekin ducks or magpie geese are common. One place had a pet jabiru stork for a while but baby agile wallabies are the norm because of the almost staple food status of their parents and a joey from the pouch quickly becomes a pet. One time the kids 'found' a baby northern nail tailed wallaby (*Onychogalea unguifera*). These are not a threatened species but they are rarely seen, and they have, as the name suggests, a claw like hardened tip to their tails. A closely related species, the bridle nail tail wallabies (*O. fraenata*) from Queensland are interesting scientists because they seem to have a remarkable immune system, effective against parasites, viruses and bacteria. Perhaps this northern species will prove of similar interest. Murray managed to talk the kids who had caught this joey into giving it to him and it eventually found its way to a foster home in Darwin and then out to the Northern Territory Wildlife Park in Berry Springs when it was older.

The Wurdeja people had a pet emu for years, which they'd raised from an egg. It had strands of red wool tied around its neck for identification and it used to walk between the outstations looking for food or company, because it liked both. Sadly, one day the wool tore or rotted off and someone shot him for food.

Animals rescued for or by the kids were always pets afterwards, though they'd rarely live for long because they'd be loved to death by the kids, the dogs would get them, or they'd starve because the correct food was never available. I sometimes thought it a little odd that people would shoot dozens of magpie geese but have a favoured goose back at camp that was perfectly safe and much loved.

No story about the Top End of Australia is complete without crocodiles. Crocodiles sell newspapers. Not literally, but Darwin's *Northern Territory News* loves them and they appear almost weekly on the front page. The paper was so reliable that in 1997 I bet my mate Steve $10 a week that there'd be a lead article about them during the 20 week school semester each and every week. He bet me $10 that there wouldn't be. At the end of the time we tallied up the score. He owed me $100 and I owed him $100, so for that semester crocs made the headlines once a fortnight and I made no extra cash. Let down by the *NT News*!

When I was growing up stories of crocodiles read like *Boy's Own* adventure stories. They were exotic monsters who outlived the dinosaurs and were masters of their domain. I knew to "never smile at a crocodile" from about the same time I learnt to walk. I used to watch nature programs about crocodiles eating wildebeests and zebra in Africa and read Willard Price adventure novels about his 19 year old protagonist named Hal, and his 15 year old brother, catching five meter giants in spite of their tender years.

Even after I arrived in the Territory and got to know a few, they loomed large in my psyche. I read all the books written by the pioneering characters of the Territory and imagined that crocodiles were so thick in the water you could practically use them as stepping stones to cross creeks. But in the early 1980s crocodiles were a newly protected species and were recovering from the hunting of previous decades so my imagination proved a little inflated.

In fact, in those days you were less likely to find big ones than you are today as they've had many years of protected growth since, though some were still out there, of course. I saw the tail of a giant once, in Jabiluka Billabong as we came around the bend in a four meter tinny. Just the tail, as it disappeared to the depths, and we swore afterwards that what we saw was bigger than the boat. The croc must have been a good five or six meters long, or to put it a more local way, 30 cm between the eyes. Aboriginal people traditionally describe crocs using two hands in the same way AFL umpires signal goals from between the center posts. They estimate the size of the croc by the distance between the eyes – a good and sensible method as the eyes and nostrils are often the only part of the crocodile you see.

Anyway, because they were mainly small in those days they were less dangerous, right? That's what Rob and I told ourselves in 1983 as we worked for Dr Rick Shine of Sydney University, collecting data on file snakes. File snakes are aquatic snakes with loose, rough skin they use to grip fish as they struggle. They are not venomous and won't bite, and they hang around the roots of *pandanus* trees along the edge of waterways or among *Nymphaea* water lily stems in flood plains. To catch them you reach in and grope among the roots and feel for their rough skins, then just pull them out. This is all very efficient and easy but a little nerve wracking as it was just as easy to grab hold of a sleeping fish which reacted very differently, giving us heart stopping moments of fright.

Rob and I caught hundreds of file snakes in this way, measuring and branding them with a soldering iron before releasing them. The number of recaptures over time would give the university an estimation of their total population. One day at Nankeen Billabong in Kakadu National Park I pulled out a ball of snakes – one giant female with nine smaller males wrapped around it trying to mate. As I called Rob for help it felt like I had a strangle hold on Medusa. I climbed up the bank and snakes were everywhere. One of their heads swung passed my leg and somehow a tooth scratched me. I maintain that I am the only person ever to have survived a file snake bite. I am probably the only one ever to have been 'bitten' at all.

We radio tracked a couple of file snakes from a billabong just down from Mudginberry Station Homestead. Dr Shine surgically inserted radio transmitters about the size of my thumb just under the skin of two large snakes. Then with the *beep beep beep* of our receiver and a little boat we located them every four hours day and night for two weeks. We also had the chance to dive down to observe them with a 'hooker' air pump in the boat above. The water was crystal clear and it was like swimming in an aquarium. The roots of *pandanus* dropped from the surface like stalactites in a cave. Archer fish, long toms, rainbow fish, saratoga, small barramundi, eel tailed catfish and others, swam among the roots or darted quickly into them as we floated by. Once, a pig nosed tortoise swam swiftly away, unwilling to risk a confrontation. Giant logs from long dead *Melaleuca* paper bark trees lay on the bottom and long thin stems of *Nymphaea* water lilies reached from the mud of the bottom to open their large flat leaves on the surface, looking from underneath like Japanese paper umbrellas. Diving here was great fun! We even saw small crocs lying on the bottom, looking at the strange new addition to billabong life trailing streams of bubbles and a plastic hose that came down from the boat above. They never seemed any threat to us.

We went to the murky Corroborree Billabong near Darwin and there were so many file snakes there that we caught over 70 in a single hour. There were crocs there too of course. They were seen often by fisherman, and would sometimes take barramundi which had been hooked before the angler could land them. But we figured that if we were quiet and calm we could collect our snakes and get out of there before the crocodiles were aware - justifying to ourselves that risks *had* to be taken for the sake of science.

We worked as a team, chatting in whispers. We each had a large plastic drum which would float behind us as we groped among the *pandanus* roots, neck deep in the muddy water.

A couple of blokes motored slowly by in a small aluminium 'tinny', towing lures from two rods that reached skywards like antennae. The driver noticed us under the pandanus clump.

"What the fuck are you blokes doing?"

"Fishing," I replied.

He changed his course slightly to travel wide of us, for which I was grateful as I really didn't want to be dragged through the billabong with a *nilsmaster* lure imbedded in me. He mumbled something to his mate, but the only words I understood were, "Crazy fucking dickheads."

Rob was a little behind me and as I worked along a *pandanus* clump I came to an inlet about three meters wide. I crossed it to reach the next clump of roots. Rob crossed a little later and when he bumped his leg against a log he raised his foot to step over it, but it was no longer there. It hadn't been there when I had crossed either and to this day Rob swears he walked into a crocodile. Taking discretion as the better part of valour, and as we already had about 120 snakes, we decided that that was enough for the day. I don't think anyone is stupid enough to do scientific research in this way anymore. Some ten years later Dr Shine's work made it into the pages of *Australian Geographic* magazine. The article mentioned Rob but, to my chagrin, not me.

I only ever actually caught two crocodiles. One was certainly caught illegally because a mate of mine in Katherine, Mick, had been fishing for barramundi with what he called 'square hooks'. He had strung a gill net across a little billabong not far out of town on the Katherine River. A small croc had got there in the net. It was thrashing about and clearly too much for one bloke to handle. So he came and got me.

"You're the biology teacher," Mick said, "You know how to catch a crocodile."

I wasn't sure of his logic but it seemed a bit of fun so off we set. He had a small punt tied to the bank and we pushed out and rowed to where he had left the net. There were floats, but no crocodile. We pulled the net up and from the weight we knew it was still entangled and it came to the surface a few centimeters from where I was sitting in the boat.

"You must have drowned it," I said. It certainly looked dead, and was badly tangled and may have been underwater for an hour.

We decided to at least untangle it so I pulled it into the boat and dropped it on the tin floor at my feet. It was about a meter and a half long and incredibly beautiful Almost black with sculpted scales the length of its body, its long scutes rising in lines down the centre of its back. Mick was mortified that he had killed something so extraordinary.

We rowed to the bank and dragged the croc up to where we could unwind the net. The body was easy to clear but untangling his snout took nearly ten minutes. Then, as soon as the last strands of nylon came away there was an explosion of life. The croc leapt up, twisted round and was back in the water and gone in the blink of an eye. We were amazed. How did it know it was untied? It must have become exhausted trying to get free and there'd been no sign of life right up to the time it jumped back into the billabong.

The second time I was involved in capturing a crocodile was in central Arnhem Land where I had spent the afternoon with Tommy Steele's family dragging a floodplain for tiger prawns. We did this often after school in the early dry season. The drag nets were 12 meters long and we'd walk through knee deep water on the flood plain with one person at each end pulling the net, and the kids on the outside splashing and making noise to drive any prawns into the path of the net.

One day we pulled up the net and a two meter croc, surrounded by large flipping prawns, slid quietly into the shallows with the net. We had dragged about 200 meters of the flood plain and it hadn't moved when the net had collected it so we were surprised to say the least. It just lay there and stared at us indignantly, despite the kids shouting and running around excitedly. I was pulling in the end of the net nearest the croc's tail and managed to flick the net over so it was no longer trapped. It then just slowly moved off back into the water.

I was back out there a few weeks later and asked Tommy about it. He said they had killed it in the end as they'd caught it a few more times in the net and it was a danger.

"He was proper cheeky," he said. "No worry though, plenty people eat him."

People would eat fresh crocodile eggs too. In the days when I used the school boat to access Marrkolidjban outstation, people would always jump aboard for lifts to or from Maningrida and they would ask me to stop at new nests along the banks of the river to raid them. Television shows go on about how dangerous this is as the new mother was supposed to be zealously guarding the nest, but I never saw any crocodiles at all during a nest raid.

Once I went with Tommy Steele and his family fishing for giant catfish on the Blyth River. Small kids were pulling in fork tailed catfish that weighed about as much as they did. The tide was out and five meters of mud stretched from the bank to the edge of the water. My little dog, Turkey, and I went off for a walk with my rifle while the fish were being cooked. Turkey was a white fluffy poodle thing, as game as Ned Kelly, but was as unlikely a bush dog as anyone ever saw in Arnhem Land. We came across a small agile wallaby which I shot for dinner – and which Turkey immediately 'brought down', tough little hunter as he was. There was a lot of blood and Turkey was covered in it by the time I reached him and the wallaby. I carried it back to camp and someone started to prepare it to cook whilst I took Turkey down to the river to wash him. At low tide I had to plough through knee deep mud to get to the edge of the water, a task that was slow and laborious. Then sometime during the process of washing him I looked up. Heading directly towards me across the river were the snout and eyes of a large crocodile, easily seen because of the large V shaped wake it left behind. It dropped under the surface just as I saw it, to make its final attack run.

Without thinking I picked Turkey up and threw him as far as I could over the mud towards the bank. He was safe but his big idiot boss was stuck knee deep in heavy mud at the water's edge like an offering to the gods. I was lucky; the croc was never seen again. Very lucky, it seems, as the next year Helen Matthews, the head nurse at Maningrida Clinic, was attacked and badly bitten in a similar situation. She slipped back in the mud in a mad scramble to get up the bank straight into the jaws of a croc. She survived but has some great scars from the experience. Tragically, a couple of years after this a young boy was not so lucky and was killed and eaten not far from the spot we had been fishing.

One of my students, Sean, survived an attack of his own one day in the swamps near Ji-balbal. He was magpie goose hunting with his father, the local church minister. The swamp was a large heavily reeded flood plain with channels of water still running through it and thousands of magpie geese feeding on the *rakai* ('water chestnuts' - corms of the spike rush, *Eloecharis dulcis*) buried in the mud. When the geese and the whistling ducks and other water birds all took to the air at once the sky would darken with their sheer numbers.

The hunting usually consisted of shooting at birds down one end of the flood plain. The whole flock would then lift off and fly to the other end and land again. The hunters would pick up any they had brought down and walk down the plain to where the birds had settled and try again. A good stalker could move slowly through the reeds and get within three or four meters before being noticed by the birds, and Sean was still learning these skills. In the old days people hunted by throwing sticks which would bring birds to the ground with broken wings, but shot guns were more productive. Residents of Top End communities are used to Land Cruiser utes filled to the brim with fresh magpie geese arriving in town for distribution in the hunting season. In the early years at Maningrida there was a truck called the 'goose truck' whose sole purpose was to collect bush tucker such as geese for the community.

Apparently Sean had picked up a shot goose in shallow water just before a small croc had come to collect it, so he was attacked instead. The croc leapt out of the water and grabbed Sean, who managed to stay on his feet, and his pious father Dudley, an ordained minister, called out,

"Stand still, Sean, and the Lord will save you."

Obediently, Sean just stood there. The croc let go and swam off.

The first I knew of it was when I saw him on the TV news - being interviewed by ABC about the experience while lying in bed in Darwin hospital. His torso was wrapped in more bandages than Tutankhamen, but as he spoke I was amazed to hear him use clear and concise, grammatically correct English – vastly different from the broken English lingo he used in his home community. He was also on the front page of the NT News, because, as I said, crocodiles sell newspapers.

Crocodiles really fancy dogs. In coastal towns like Maningrida dogs playing on the beach are prime targets for dinner. I used to joke that Turkey was my crocodile insurance – I always reckoned a croc would take him instead of me if we were in the wrong spot, even if he was only a little thing. I knew a much bigger dog named Bear, a Rottweiler of some 70 kg. He, his owner and his girlfriend of some 50kg, were fishing one night on the Maningrida barge landing. It was dark, there was a splash and the dog was gone, without a whimper.

The Maningrida police trapped this crocodile before he upgraded his diet to include children and he was strapped to a board ready to be shipped to a Darwin croc farm. We teachers, never ones to let an opportunity pass, took the kids up to see all four meters of his scaly length. The police sergeant wasn't amused to hear us standing around singing the ABC's *Play School* theme song, "There's a bear in there…"

The artist Clifton Pugh (no relation) had visited Maningrida many years before and people still talked of the way he used to go skinny dipping off the same barge landing where this couple were fishing that night. His luck held out, it seems.

Crocodiles are a part of life if you're outdoors in the Top End of Australia and crocodile attacks can be and sometimes are, fatal. Many people who have been attacked, and many who have ended up dead, have been locals who should have known better about where they were and what they were doing.

People have been attacked when they were fishing knee deep in water in a tidal estuary at dusk. Val Plumwood made the news when she hit a croc with her canoe in shallow water in the East Alligator River. She capsized and was attacked but bravely crawled two kilometers to the ranger station. A German tourist was eaten when swimming at midnight in Airport Billabong in Kakadu, after being told by her tour guide that it was safe. Kerry McLaughlan, a storeman from the Ranger Uranium Mine, who had been in the Top End for decades, was killed by a large crocodile we knew as Eric when fishing at the East Alligator River ford of Cahill's Crossing, at a place he'd fished hundreds of times before. Perhaps people living with danger become a bit blasé about it. Eric used to chase dogs in the days when people were allowed to camp beside the river, and he was seen several times wandering among the tents late at night.

Jokes about attacks quickly do the rounds.

"Have you heard how crocodiles prefer their Americans with ginger?" came out the day after the tragic death of an American model named Ginger in the Kimberleys.

Tasteless torn T-shirts with dyed red stains around the tears and the words 'I survived the NT' or similar are very popular souvenirs in Darwin, and from the croc farms you can buy such useful items as crocodile foot back scratchers, or the pair of croc head bookends no study should be without.

Crocodiles are not dangerous to everyone and most people are lucky to even see one. However, I reckon there must be a mathematical equation that will take in the size of the croc and relate it in inverse proportion to the stupidity of an individual. I have a photograph of a father watching over his children swimming at Cahill's Crossing. He was sitting just below a 'BEWARE – saltwater crocodiles inhabit these waters' sign. You could take their ignorant behaviour and throw in a luck differential and it'll give you a likelihood of your death by croc. The actuaries had it – a few years ago you could buy a life insurance policy for just $10 against a croc attack, so someone knew the numbers.

A baby crocodile business started in Maningrida a few years after I left. The community took out a license to harvest eggs from riverside nests up the Liverpool River, and would incubate them in a big shed near the police station. I visited them one afternoon when I was back for a few weeks in 2003. Matthew Ryan, an ex student who had left school to become a police aid (but who then worked as a ranger), showed me around the shed.

"This is where we put the eggs," he told me while pulling a drawer out of a large incubator that reminded me of a pottery kiln. There were dozens of them. Each had a pencil line drawn on the top. The incubator was noisy: this was no quiet nursery, as a large compressor kept it at just the right temperature.

"What's that line for?" I asked over the din.

"When we dig them out of the nest we mark which side is up. If they go in here upside down they will die," replied Matthew. "Come and see the babies."

In another tray were some hatchlings.

"These are all males," he said. "Their eggs were all incubated to 34 degrees. If you make them colder, 30 or 31 degrees, the babies all come out female."

The babies were chirping. *Errng, Errng.*

"Can I borrow one to get a photo?"

Matthew handed me a random baby. I grasped him around his body and took him outside with my camera. He was a feisty little thing, not at all happy, and he would have bitten me if he'd had a chance.

Matthew explained that all the hatchlings were due to fly out the next day to go to a crocodile farm in Queensland. They would all survive and grow to be a meter or two in comparative luxury before being skinned to become someone's shoes or a handbag, or served up on a plate in some swanky restaurant. In the wild only one or two of every hundred make it to their first birthday. The others fall prey to predators ranging from jabiru storks to other crocodiles and big fish, so one could say that these little fellows were the lucky ones.

Crocodiles have been protected now for more than 30 years and they are growing bigger each year – both in terms of size and population. Through publicity of attacks and the efforts of rangers and others in moving them from picnic areas and beaches, Top Enders are at least educated about the dangers and can make their choices after that. Even so, the *NT News* regularly prints photos of idiots larking about on the steel croc traps in Darwin Harbour – offering tastier baits than the usual dead feral pig or fish heads. Now, for a few dollars, tourists can cage dive in an aquarium with crocodiles in Mitchell Street, in the centre of Darwin city, or visit croc farms. They can also eat them at restaurants and, in fact, many more crocodiles get eaten by people these days than people get eaten by crocodiles.

7

BUSH TUCKER

"Derek, you got your shot gun? Let's go."

Kevin Jawugurr was the head man in Yilan. A big bloke with wild curly hair, he and I would sometimes go fishing in the afternoon, but this was the first time he had invited me out at night. In fact, it was well after dark but the moon was full and its warm pastel glow lit the flood plains but cast deep shadows into the forest. I piled in the back of his Land Cruiser ute with a bunch of kids and we headed off into the bush. Kevin's beat-up old truck had only one dim headlight working and we moved slowly along the track at the back of the dunes using moonlight as much as the headlight to navigate. He was heading to a large tree he knew of which was heavily laden with flowers. We heard it before we saw it.

Hundreds of fruit bats were squabbling over the flowers. Pollen and bits of torn petal and broken twigs fell down like snow. There were bats flying everywhere. They stood out beautifully against the

After school hunting party from Ji-Marda School – I'd learn Burarra, the kids would learn English.

bright night sky, their wings shiny in the moonlight, but they flew so quickly I had little faith we'd be able to hit them at night and told Kevin so. We only had about six shot gun shells between us.

"No worries," he said, "Watch."

He took my shot gun and loaded both barrels then walked under the tree. He stood quietly for a while, raised the shotgun and fired straight at the moon through the tree with both barrels. Little brown and black bodies dropped out of the trees. Two shots and Kevin had a bucket full with about 20 bats.

We took them back to Yilan and cooked them on a fire outside the school. Kevin burned off the leathery wings and the fur first, then cut the bats open to remove the meat. About the only meat on a bat is the breast - the chest muscles it uses for flying. These he barbequed on an old piece of tin and we sat around the fire to eat them. They are best described as 'gamey' with strong flavoured dark meat, perhaps a little chewy, but I found them nice enough and ate as many pieces as I could get that evening.

Bats were easy to stomach, but there were foods that I never did get the courage to try - mangrove worms for one, which many people cherished. We used to find them on mud mussel trips down along the Blyth River.

The Wurdeja people were very partial to mud mussels, which they called *an-bombala*. These mussels bury themselves in the ground deep inside mangrove forests. We used to drive down to the banks of the Blyth River where there were extensive stretches of mangroves which were always high and dry at low tide. The mud was firm underfoot, not like in the mangroves along the coast, which would see me sink to me knees. Here I could walk easily, stepping over tangles of aerial roots and skirting around the gnarled trunks of ancient trees. It took me ages to find any of our quarry, though some of the kids were expert at spotting them. Esau tried to teach me.

"Look, see that line?" he said, pointing to a faint straight line in the mud. It proved to be the lips of a black shell. He took a stick and prized out a large mussel about the size of a small apple. Eventually I got the hang of it and proudly returned to the dinner camp with three large mussels. I placed them carefully on the pile of a hundred or so the kids had found in the same time. Most of the mussels were then laid in lines on the ground and a quick burning fire of dry grass and thin sticks was lit on top of them. Within minutes the shells had opened and they were cooked and ready to eat. They make really good eating.

We'd go hunting for mussels quite regularly but as always when you're hunting with Aboriginal people, they would also be looking for other things to eat. One afternoon I could hear an axe being used up ahead. I clambered through the mangroves, always much slower than everyone else, and found Georgina Mason in a small clearing. She was hacking into a huge old mangrove tree which had a few large branches clearly dead and rotting.

"Here it is," she exclaimed at last. With a stick she hooked and started to pull out a purple tube worm about a meter long. This was a mangrove worm and Georgina assured me it was "really good tucker."

"How do you cook it?" I asked.

"You don't cook it, you eat it raw like this." With that she took a section of it about 20 centimeters long and put one end in her mouth. Being tubes, mangrove worms are full of the mud and wood debris upon which they feed. Georgina place two fingers around the worm and ran them down its body, squeezing out the mud like some swamp toothpaste. Then she just sucked the worm in like spaghetti and smacked her lips.

"Gun-mola mola," she said. "Good." I have had to take her word for it. Mangrove worms looked, to me, about the most unappetizing of all bush tucker and I never tried them.

Georgina was a good bush cook and she knew how to get edible food out of the strangest of places. Cycad palms are prehistoric slow growing hardy palms only a meter or two high, scattered through the *martay* forests of Arnhem Land. Apparently they only grow about a centimeter each year, so a two meter specimen was a seedling when Matthew Flinders passed along the coast here. Cycads bear clusters of brown plum-sized fruit which, unfortunately for the casual grazer are toxic until the poison is removed.

After I'd dropped the Ji-malawa kids home and was returning to Wurdeja for the afternoon one day, Georgina, who had come along for the ride, asked me to stop in an area of forest thick with cycads. In a few minutes she'd filled a dilly bag with the fruit and back at Wurdeja she put them in a flour tin of water to soak.

Soaking leaches out the poisons, but it takes days. I was back the next Monday and they'd been soaking for the whole weekend. Cooking was simply boiling but the resulting mass had to be kneaded by hand, wrapped in paper bark and then have the liquid squeezed out of it before it was ready. I was keen to try it and eagerly joined the kids as it was unwrapped.

"We call it *ngitja*," said Georgina as she handed me a piece wrapped in paper bark. I reeled backwards. It smelled like something you'd find in a baby's nappy!

"You can't eat this," I complained to roars of laughter from the kids. "It stinks!"

But the kids were readily munching away so I mustered my courage and gave it a go.

Rarely in my experience have the smell and taste of a food been so far apart. *Ngitju* is indeed a good bush tucker – it reminded me a little of nougat for some reason, though it wasn't sweet. It was chewy and filling and like nothing I had eaten before, but its smell would kill a brown dog.

In Maningrida one day I thought I heard a baby crying on the beach. I investigated to find not a baby, but a dugong which had been speared and tied to the rocks. Some people had been out hunting dugongs and had managed to catch two. They are very large marine beasts so to butcher both would have provided so much meat that a lot of it would have become rotten before it was eaten, so the hunters had tied this poor animal up to save for later. They arrived to butcher it whilst I was there in fact, and I asked them what it tasted like.

"Maynmak, really good tucker," was the reply, but it always is when you ask about bush tucker.

Later that afternoon one of the guys surprised me by knocking on my door. He had a piece of cooked dugong for me and a small plastic bag of meat. He pushed the cooked piece into my hand.

"Go on, try," he said, "You never know if you don't."

It smelled really good so I did indeed eat it and relished it. It has a funny fluffy rubbery consistency and was hard to identify.

"What is it?" I asked.

"It's the guts." He said. Dugong tripe!

He left the meat with me to cook up later, and

I fully intended to, but it was in the fridge so long I eventually gave it to the dog.

—————————————

Wurdeja was always a particularly good place to be at the end of the wet season. In May, as the coastal floodplains 15 or so kilometers to the west were drying up, we'd go prawning after school. There was usually a truck load of us – a bunch of kids, a few women and the old man, Tommy. The track through the bush was narrow and the forest contained large numbers of billy-goat plum trees, famous for the very high vitamin C content of the fruit. The first stop would be to collect these so we were already eating by the time the forest opened up to broad floodplains. At this early dry season time of year the quarry was always tiger prawns, although a smaller species of prawn was common as well. Along the rivers and around the mangroves the large local *Aedes* species of mosquitoes have striped bodies. They are easy to recognize and Burarra people call them *janbul*. Tiger prawns look like giant janbul, striped with long legs, so it only stands to reason that they are called *janbul janbul*. They are as big as bananas.

The last remaining areas of water on the flood plains were almost snag-free and we could pull long drag-nets through the shallows for a hundred meters or more at a time. We'd quickly catch bucket loads of prawns, take them back to our dinner camp and cook them in the coals of a fire or boil them in a billy. We would feast until it was hard to move then we'd watch the sun slowly set over the flood plains before making our weary way back to Wurdeja.

What an amazing place the flood plains are. They are actually strings of very shallow depressions which dry out into clay pans by about June each year. Even when full of water the mud bottoms are almost vegetation free but occasional *Melaleuca* paper bark trees and clumps of fresh water mangroves mark the less salty areas. The *Melaleuca* are useful trees in the bush: their bark can be pulled off and used to wrap food, as a table cloth on the ground, or to start fires when everything else around is wet. The small swamp species are also often festooned with orchids, the sap of which was traditionally used for the glue in body painting and the early bark paintings.

The flooded areas are surrounded by grasslands but because occasional salt water flows in from the spring tides the billabongs are too salty for the grass and reeds to survive, which is why they remain mostly clear of snags for the drag nets. While we dragged them for the prawns, the kids would disappear into the flood plains for hours and return with baby burdekin ducks, blue herons or brolgas to play with and keep as pets. This was also the place where, one afternoon, we dragged up the crocodile which was as much a surprise to us as it was to the croc.

When the floodplains were dry enough we could drive across them to get to Gumugumuk to go crabbing in the mangroves. My role on crabbing expeditions was quickly explained to me. As I was too heavy and would sink in the mud in these mangroves I was relegated to collect fire wood and sit in the shade of the big tamarind tree on the beach with the old men and small children. The beach was short, no more than two hundred meters long, and looking out past some small uninhabited islands a part of larger Milingimbi Island could be seen in the distance.

So, while we sat in the shade everyone else quickly disappeared into the mangroves where I could not go. The women and kids, long accustomed to the mangroves and knowing where to put their feet to get support from hidden underground roots, would practically run through the trees pulling crabs out of their holes by the dozen. Georgina and Dalma were particularly skilled at crabbing and would return with a sack full to the brim within an hour or so.

Mud crabs are famous in the Territory. They are as big as a dinner plate with two large claws which can snap a careless finger effortlessly. The ladies would pull them from their holes and hit them with a stick and knock these claws off, then pick up the crab with impunity. Like the prawns, we'd cook them in the coals of the fire or boil them in a billy. The large claws when cooked can be cracked open and the meat revealed. They looked like paddlepops – ice creams on a stick - and were very good eating indeed. I rarely ate the bodies as it was a lot of work to get to the meat but, inexplicably, others would prefer the bodies to the claws.

One day Tommy Steele and I were sitting in the shade watching the beach. Rowan and a couple of other little kids were playing in the sand and we were eating a stingray Tommy had speared earlier.

He had boiled the ray's meat and rolled it into balls, for a peculiar consistency and flavor and, although I thought it was odd food indeed and was a gritty with beach sand, it was quite pleasant.

Suddenly down the other end of the beach a wallaby burst from the scrub and went straight into the sea. A dingo appeared hot on his heals but at the kids' shouts he turned tail. The wallaby swam out to sea in a big arc and returned to the beach. Rowan, a six year old, led the small kids out to meet it in the shallows and quickly captured it. By the time the ladies returned from crabbing it was boiling in a flour drum of water on the fire, its legs sticking upwards, its cut off tail buried in hot coals. This was truly a land of plenty.

Bush tucker trips to Gumugumuk on some occasions were also shopping trips when the Cabbage Patch Man was about. Peter the Cabbage Patch Man got his name because he had seven children. They all lived on an old coastal trading boat and ran a mobile shop for local people to buy groceries, junk food and equipment. Every six months or so he used to moor off the coast at Gumugumuk and when we arrived would come and pick us up in his dinghy. We'd all pile in and go shopping. Sometimes we'd gather up all his kids with ours and play sports on the beach.

The Cabbage Patch Man and his family had an amazing life, though tragedy struck when one of his sons jumped into the water at Milingimbi and impaled himself on a metal post someone had left standing in the mud. Peter gave up the nomad seafarer's way after that and we never heard any more of him.

Gamardi Outstation had a magpie goose wandering around when I was visiting one week. The goose was quite tame as someone had taken it from a nest and brought it back to the outstation where it lived on bread and rice for a few months as a much loved pet, along with a baby wallaby or two and a dozen mangy dogs.

I was camping in my house as usual. A magnificent sunset lit up the western sky with hues of reds, yellows and blues and, as it was getting dark I walked up and sat with Margaret and Michael. Kathleen and Nina and some of the boys were there too. Five or six other fires were already lit among the houses and humpies and groups of people sat around their fires, enjoying the sunset and each other's company.

I noticed a few people sat with shot guns across their laps. There was nothing too unusual about that but as it got darker I found out why. In the distance we could hear a series of honks.

"They're coming," Michael whispered.

"Who?" I asked.

Suddenly, lines of low flying geese appeared moving west. I could see them against the last cobalt blue of the sky. There were V formations of about 20 birds each flying just above tree height, like spitfires returning home after a day's battle. The clear strip of land which ran from the community down to the river might have been funneling them this way but it was clear that Gamardi was built under the flight path for hundreds of magpie geese, moving from the Jibalbal floodplains across the river to wherever they roosted for the night.

"Bang!"

"Bang!"

Like flack guns in an air raid, a half dozen double-barreled shot guns opened fire. Geese fell all around us and once again I was impressed about how productive this land could be. The barrage only lasted a minute or two but there was suddenly enough fresh meat for the entire community for a couple of days.

One hapless goose, apparently really keen to be cooked, actually landed in a fire.

Gamardi was only about 13 kilometers from Wurdeja but there were marked differences in the types of hunting activities each community was involved with. Occasionally Gamardi would join Wurdeja and go to the salt water area around Gumugumuk for prawns, but more likely they'd go to their own inland country where small floodplains fed by the Yurunga Creek were surrounded by the forest. Once, Young Michael took me and a bunch of kids east to a remote area in search of a buffalo.

We drove for half an hour or so through the forest on wheel tracks that couldn't have been used more than once or twice a year. We came to a more open area where dark grey 'magnetic' termite hills aligned themselves east-west to avoid the sun's direct rays. A fire had gone through months before and the grass had returned, short and green like a lawn. There were thousands of termite hills stretching as far as we could see, looking like some gothic cemetery. I wouldn't have been surprised to see a bunch of people in black suits standing around a newly dug grave.

Most of the trees here were salmon gums with their white and pink trunks, billy goat plums or *Melaleuca* or bush apple trees. There were occasional stands of *Livistonia* sand palms and cycads and thick areas of the purple flowered *Callitrix* 'turkey' bush between them. The flood plain was a little north of where we stopped and apart from some buffalo damage in the form of well padded foot paths and a few wallows among the reeds, it seemed amazingly pristine country. Although feral pigs were common in western Arnhem Land in the 1990s, they had yet to reach this area. The only feral animals I saw here were buffalos and the ubiquitous cat. Sadly, I believe pigs have since conquered this area too and it is likely cane toads are there, or soon will be, in their inexorable march across the country.

Michael and another bloke with a gun moved off in one direction towards the swamp and, so I wouldn't spoil their chances, I left the kids at the truck and loaded my shot gun and took a different direction with my dog, Turkey. I skirted around the wetlands looking for geese or ducks but nothing presented itself so I walked back to the truck in a giant circle, returning to it from the south. The kids we'd left at the truck were amazed.

"This isn't your country! How come you know where to go? Where you been?"

"I have an excellent sense of direction," I replied. In truth the truck had been easy to find in the bush. The kids had been skylarking and made so much noise I could hear them from over a kilometer away, but I didn't tell them that.

We waited for Michael to come back and spent the time mining holes in the termite mounds. Some were two meters tall and perhaps a meter wide, but so thin the kids could drill a hole from one side to the other with a stick. Half an hour of this and a giant termite hill looked more like a sculpture of grey Swiss cheese.

Eventually Michael returned, unfortunately also empty handed, and we all piled into the truck to return home before dark.

We hadn't been going for five minutes when we came across a bull buffalo walking along the track in front of us. A single shot from Michael's .303 brought it down, and a second made sure it was dead. If that that wasn't good enough Turkey latched onto its ear and gave it a determined shaking. It was good shooting – in my time as a ranger I shot a number of buffalos and I knew if the shot wasn't perfect the buffalo would just run off.

As it got dark, Michael and I butchered the beast by the light of the truck, amid clouds of mosquitoes attracted by the blood and a million other insects attracted by the lights. We took the hind quarters and all the 'ribeye' or scotch fillet – those long muscles down each side of the spine. It was more than enough to feed everyone back at Gamardi.

At Marrkolidjban after school we'd sometimes go swimming in the local creeks or just wander along through the bush to see what turned up. One day I was talking to Charlie and Margo about file snakes as we walked barefoot through a *Melaleuca* swamp north of the community, with their kids scampering ahead of us.

"What's the name for file snakes in Kunwinjku?"

"*Bekka*," replied Charlie at exactly the same time as some kids running ahead of us shouted.

"*Bekka, bekka!*"

We ran up and the kids had already pulled out the large female file snake from a small water hole. One of the boys killed it by placing its head in his mouth, biting down and pulling until the snake's neck broke. We cooked it later for an afternoon snack by boiling it in a tin of water and the meat came out in long fat ropes. Moist and delicious, it was the best tasting meat I'd had for a long time.

Like Wurdeja and Gamardi, the forest around Marrkolidjban was full of food. Sometimes I'd wander down to the creek at dusk with my shot gun, and spot a magpie goose settling into a tree to roost for the night. It was a simple matter to shoot it and take it back and barbeque it on the coals of my fire. If there were no geese it didn't take long to hook a fish from the creek.

Most days the local men would just walk out into the bush and come back an hour later with an agile wallaby, a euro, a sand goanna or an emu for dinner. In *sugar bag* season people would tie a tiny bit of spider's web to a captured native bee to make it easy to see, release it and follow it as it went home, then raid the honey from a hive hidden in a tree hollow. The women would easily find wild yams growing underground and they'd also collect shellfish, tortoises and water lily bulbs from the wetlands.

In the early wet season it was common to spot *Chlamydosaurus,* the frill necked lizards. These are large dragon lizards, perhaps 80 cm long, which spend most of their time camouflaged in trees, but in November and December they can be seen running on two legs on the ground between trees. Their frills are large collars of skin which they hold folded back along the neck, but when they're courting or alarmed they spread them wide and gape open their mouths displaying red, yellow, orange, black and pink scales. Although they can run quite fast they can also be easy to catch. They will often stand their ground with a threat display designed to scare you off, so it's just a matter of picking them up, but if they run and reach a tree they will quickly climb out of reach.

I met Zoe Morgan and a bunch of her students from Mankorlod on the road one day. They had spotted a *blanket* lizard, as they called it, and it had climbed a tree. It was quite high but sensibly now motionless as, with its frill held tightly against its neck, it looked more like a branch than a lizard. The kids were in the process of throwing sticks at it to try and knock it down. As Zoe and I were chatting a Land Cruiser came along, driven by Big John, a senior man from Mankorlod and the father of some of the kids.

"What you looking at?"

"Blanket lizard, up there."

Big John didn't get out of his car but leaned out

the window to look up.

"Wait," he said. A second later the barrel of a shot gun came through the window. Still sitting in the car he held the gun out of the window with one hand, pointed it in the general direction of the lizard and fired. The lizard fell to the ground; Big John nodded a farewell and disappeared down the track. The lizard was in the cooking fire within an hour.

In the outstations people were always eating wherever we went. If we walked anywhere during the wet season when the grass grew high the kids would pick long stems of a grass they called 'sugar cane' and suck its sweet juice, or we'd pick fruit of the billy goat plum tree (*anmorlak*). Near the Mumeka flood plains there were large areas of a bush called *manjulukun*, which carried masses of tiny sweet dark purple berries which were favourites of the kids. Emus like the berries too so it was a good place to hunt for them. A good hunter can call an emu close enough to shoot with a deep guttural booming sound because they are curious birds. I saw a bloke try to attract one by hitting the bull bar of the Land Cruiser once, but on that day the bird was too smart and ran off. I accidentally knocked an emu down with my truck on the way to Marrkolidjban one morning. It ran alongside me for ages and I was just enjoying watching it, but it suddenly swerved left and dived under my wheels. I picked it up and dropped it off at Charlie and Margo's camp. They plucked it and butchered it and cooked it by boiling some and barbecuing the rest. The whole school fed on its grey meat during school break.

Near Yilan there are stands of 'rotten cheese fruit' trees, 'red apple' trees and 'green apple' trees which grow in the sandy soil beside the black soil plains, and the green plum tree *andudjmi*, which produces bunches of grape sized green fruit really popular with the children. I was never allowed to drive past a fruiting green plum tree without stopping to let the kids pick the plums by the billy load.

If we were near creeks or flood plains people would pick water lily stems and munch away whilst collecting mussels or long necked tortoises. In the dry season the lilies would be gone but in the soil were their bulbs which can be dug up and eaten raw. Tortoises are also buried in the mud over the long dry season and can be found by poking a stick into cracks in the mud whilst listening for a change of sound when a shell is tapped.

It seems everything can be eaten. I saw a taipan run over by a vehicle in front of me once and I stopped to have a look. This most dangerous of snakes was still alive and although its midsection was flattened and it was doomed, it was still fairly aggressive. It was nearly two meters long and I was curious - someone had told me they are good eating. So, to put it out of its misery and with a culinary interest in mind, I chopped its head off with my machete and gutted and skinned it. That night when we were camping, I fried long strips of taipan meat in butter in a billy can lid. It was slightly rubbery in texture but had an innocuous taste, more like the butter than meat.

Sometimes we would also use fresh road kill for

bait if we were going fishing. We used a cockatoo that I hit with a Land Cruiser once to catch catfish and it worked pretty well. Top notch pigeons were also good bait.

As a visiting teacher in Arnhem Land you can't help but be carried along on bush tucker expeditions after school and you get an opportunity to eat some pretty weird stuff. However, in Aboriginal communities across Australia diet is becoming a real issue. White flour, sugar, soft drinks, tinned bully beef and alcohol all fuel the flames of obesity, diabetes and other 'lifestyle' diseases which put even the 55 year old survivors into files marked 'elders' at the health clinic. Aborigines nowadays have a lower life expectancy than other Australians and much effort is continually needed to educate people about the dangers of poor diet, and abusing alcohol, tobacco, kava and other drugs. In the end it will always come down to choice and an educated choice is often, though not always, better.

One group who automatically have an edge are the folk who live in Arnhem Land outstations. They have a better and more traditional diet, at least partly, because the tucker truck may only come every two weeks and in the 'lean' times between shop visits people are happy to help themselves to the living larder that surrounds them.

8

TURKEY

Turkey, the little pampered pooch I have mentioned earlier, was a constant companion when I visited homelands and an ice breaker for Aboriginal people everywhere. People I'd never met previously knew his name before they knew who I was. He was a great traveler and used to sit in the Land Cruiser, boat or plane, swim across swamps or walk on hot dusty tracks equally happily.

He also had the nine lives of a cat.

One Friday after a week at Marrkolidjban I needed to leave at about 11 am for the six kilometer walk back to the Liverpool River. It usually took an hour along the rough track through the sorghum spear grass and the tide would have dropped too far to get the boat over sand bars near the river's mouth and up the barge landing at Maningrida if I'd left any later. Some of the kids and a few young men came with me for the ride to town. Turkey ran ahead and back as always – trebling the distance he actually had to go. It was late wet season and the spear grass was more than head height and grew as thick as a Mason hairbrush. The spear grass was nearly seeding and in parts the track through the bush was a green tunnel. Spear grass is not called that because it looks like a bunch of spears stuck in the ground. Rather it's the action of the seeds when they ripen and fall to the ground. The seeds 'spear' themselves into the soil by twisting their long tails as they dry out. This is quite amazing to watch. Spear grass plants are well adapted to fire and burying the seeds in the soil before fire burns the dry stems in the dry season is a great survival mechanism. The seeds are quite uncomfortable to get imbedded in your clothing however, so pushing through long spear grass patches is not a very pleasant experience. They're also one of the reasons sheep don't do well in the north – the seeds spear through a fleece as happily as leaf litter and bury themselves in flesh. Towards the end of the wet season the weather often unleashes its full fury through short lived tempests called *knock-em-down* storms, when the rain comes down hard and the winds whip around like hammers. These storms flatten the spear grass and make pushing through it even more of a challenge as it becomes horizontally tangled.

On this day we come round a bend and surprised a wallaby coming the other way. It crashed off through the bush to our left. The little apricot flash immediately after it was Turkey, yapping his high pitched bark he reserved for the maximum excitement of a chase and we heard him for ages away in the distance.

Turkey would occasionally run off after something like that, and I was used to him catching up with me when he'd had his fun. This time we reached the river before him and retrieved the boat from its mooring in the middle, using a tiny fiberglass canoe. Usually the tide had dragged the boat upstream or downstream a bit during the week and I always moored it in the center of the river so that it was never swept under the trees on the banks or among snags. A boat stuck under a tree can end up being held under and be sunk as the tide rises. Getting to it in mid river in the tiny canoe we had for the purpose was always a little dicey. There was no freeboard to spare and there were crocodiles around. I tipped in more than once during the year I used this method.

In about half an hour all the kids were loaded and waiting, but there was no sign of the little rough tough hunting dog. The tide was draining the river and we were still 30 kilometers from its mouth.

I jogged back up the track calling him but was aware of the draining tide and the need to hurry. At one point I came across his tracks re-entering the road, but he had turned the wrong way and headed back to Marrkolidjban. I didn't have the time to retrieve him, so I returned to the boat and we headed back to Maningrida.

I wasn't too worried. I knew there were people there who'd look after him and Marrkolidjban had an airstrip which was occasionally visited by the Progress Association's plane based in Maningrida. I called in to see the pilot that evening.

"Brett, if you get to go to Marrkolidjban over the weekend could you ask around to see if Turkey is there?"

"I have a run out there tomorrow" he replied, and promised he would keep a look out.

Early next morning Brett's plane buzzed my house as he returned to Maningrida. I jumped on my trail bike and went up to the airstrip in time to watch the plane taxi in. Turkey was sitting bolt upright in the front seat, the only passenger, no worse the wear for his sleep over in the bush and in fact a very welcome guest in a community of dog lovers.

He was popular wherever we went. When I first started teaching at Wurdeja the kids would run out in excitement as I drove up in my yellow Land Cruiser ute.

"Derek, Derek, Derek!" they'd be yelling. But very quickly I was a side show.

"Turkey's here. Turkey… Turkey!"

An old man at Ji-marda told me one day,

"You know, Derek, when I first bin see that dog I like him. But now… it's love!" He offered to look after him if I wanted to leave him there for holidays.

Another bloke who fell in love with Turkey was Gordon Machbirrbirr, who worked in the Literacy Production Centre in Maningrida. One night Gordon was in my house and he gave Turkey a 'naming ceremony', part of which involved Gordon wiping sweat from his armpits and rubbing it into Turkey's woolly locks.

There was always a lot of movement among the homeland schools, and this included school trips for sports. We'd either truck the kids or sometimes fly them to neighbouring communities to participate in competitions, and Turkey would always come too. We got in the habit of dying him in team colours and writing slogans on his side, and I'd give him a special haircut and shape his beard and moustache. He could look like the *Laughing Cavalier* with a goatee beard and wide mustachios or sport a pointy nosed *Speedy Gonzales* look just as easily. He was known by everyone, as far away as Gapuwiyak in the east and Gunbalanya in the west.

Turkey's nine lives were being used up in the bush and sometimes he was lucky to survive. One day when we were on the way to Gamardi he fell out of the truck and I didn't notice for almost 30 kilometers. I backtracked for so long and was just about to give up when I saw his tracks in the sand on the road. I had missed him, so I turned the truck around and followed the tracks back. After a few hundred meters I stopped again to check they were still there and noticed a second set of tracks going the other way. Turkey had chased me for a while then turned around and headed back the way we'd come towards Nemerilli Crossing on the Blyth River. I followed him that way again and sure enough within a minute or two there he was sitting in the middle of the road.

Another time I was going sailing around Melville Island with my mate, Pat. We were using my 'tinny' boat to get to his yacht which was moored off the barge landing. Because it was still early, before dawn, I'd been lazy and hadn't put up the canopy. It lay flat on its frame across the bow and made a great little nest for Turkey to sleep on. However, as I gunned the motor the wind caught it and flipped it up and

I caught a glimpse of Turkey's wide eyed mustachioed expression of astonishment as he flew through the air over my head and into the sea behind. We turned and I pulled out a very soggy dog before he became breakfast for a crocodile or a shark.

Being little didn't stop Turkey having a go at crocodiles when he could. I was riding a trail bike along the water's edge on a beach near Maningrida just before dark in the rain one time, with Turkey riding on the seat behind me. Visibility was poor and I went to the seaward side of what I had thought was a log laying on the sand. As we passed it leapt to its feet and headed to the water. I struggled to avoid a collision, and before I could do anything Turkey had jumped off the bike and was after it. The crocodile was perhaps three meters long, quite a big one, but luckily it was in the water and gone before Turkey could get to him.

He got his chance though. Turkey and I lived a few years in a beach side house in Pularumpi, on Melville Island. I could sit on my veranda and see crocs patrolling the beach. One day we heard a bang and went down to find that Harry Puruntatameri had shot a four meter, three legged crocodile not 50 meters from my front door (and in the place I used to jump in to get wet after running on the beach!) We went down to have a look and Turkey immediately attacked the corpse. I have a photograph of him biting the crocodile's nose, its cavernous jaws propped open with a stick.

Turkey was a great adventurer. In the middle of the Ji-marda floodplain there is a giant banyan tree.

It's the only shade for miles around. Its trunk was wrapped in a mass of roots and others would hang down from its branches. One hot day we stopped in its shade for lunch as I moved between schools. I was sitting quietly looking out across the plains when I heard an animal climbing high above me in the tree. It was Turkey. He had found a route up through the tangled mass of aerial roots and chased a lizard higher in the tree than is natural for a dog to go. It was much harder getting him down.

One day, further east on the flood plain we had walked out through knee deep water to visit a stand of *Corypha* palms. These are large heavy palms which are found at only two or three places in Australia so I was interested in seeing them. They only flower once, after 50 or 100 years of growing, and then they die. Several had obviously flowered as they were already dead, and their giant trunks stood tall and leafless, mute cenotaphs to the glory of reproduction.

I'd been catching eels with a few kids in a tidal creek and spotted them from a distance. As we waded through the area I noticed a large number of grass-hoppers in the reeds. The funny thing was that as we approached they would jump into the water and dive under the surface to escape! I'd never heard of grasshoppers doing this and thought I'd try and catch some, but they were quick, and we splashed around trying to get them. Turkey, up to his chest in the water, just stood and watched. A grasshopper landed in the water just in front of his nose and dived. With astonishing speed, so did he, disappearing underwater for a second. He came up with the grass hopper in his mouth, its long legs protruding from his drooping moustache. He was a bit bemused when I took it from him but I was wondering if we'd discovered a new species so preserved it and sent it to the NT Museum. I pictured it being named after Turkey, its captor, but months later I received a polite letter saying thanks, but they knew all about it already.

Turkey died a very old dog in Alice Springs many years later. He is buried under a cairn at the junction of two tributaries of the Hugh River, some 50 kilometers west of Alice. One day some lonely cattleman will come across his grave and wonder at the stone on the river bank which is carved with his name: 'Turkey'.

PHOTOS

Garmardi 1992. I took every second hand bath I found to the outstations where they quickly became swimming pools for the kids.

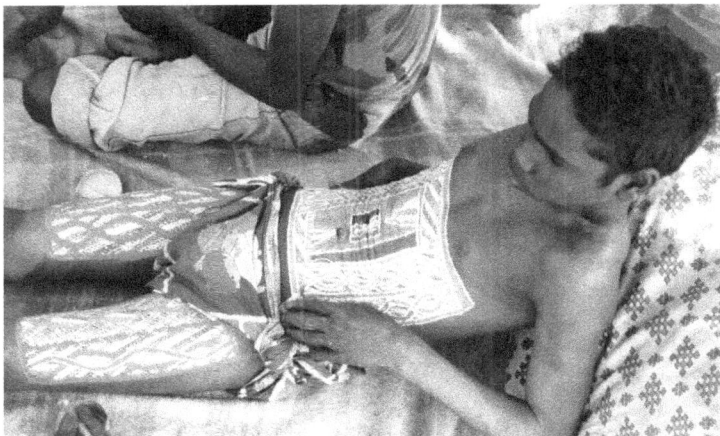

Japi initiation – the boys are painted in intricate rrark designs that can take hours to complete.

Wurdeja School 1990 – our end of term Christmas party.

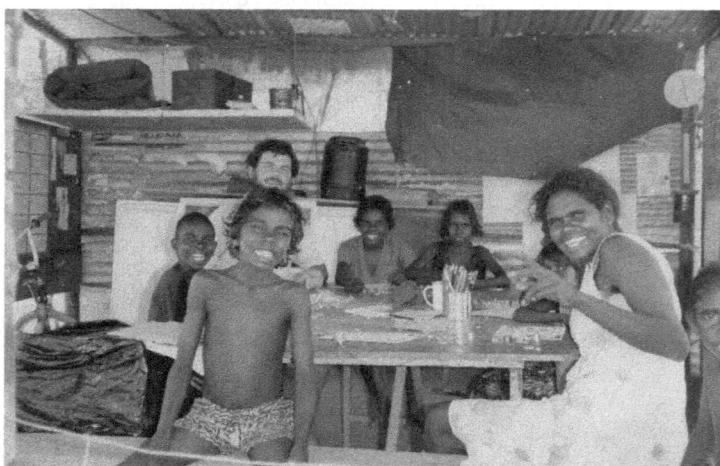

Wurdeja School 1992, Georgina Mason on the right was an excellent teacher, despite having low literacy herself she could motivate children to learn well.

The japi initiation is a family event and everyone lines up happily for group photos to mark the rites of passage.

Antelopine kangaroo being cooked.

Japi initiation: Quincy Carter, painted by Johnny Bulanbulan at his japi in 1993

An antelopine kangaroo at Ji-Marda. Leon Ali, at 15, was already a skilled hunter

Wurdeja Outstation 1993

Catching catfish in the Blyth River at low tide.

Ji-Marda School 1991

9

WEEKENDS

Life in Maningrida was fairly social – both with the local people and with the other Balanda who lived in town. Both groups liked to party, but people partied in such different ways there were only a few who regularly attended both types of parties. In general, if alcohol was involved, most Balanda would stay away from the locals' parties and funnily enough, vice versa. The exceptions were events like school staff get-togethers and barbeques where all the staff would come along, have a few beers and generally be very well behaved.

Often the Balanda parties were 'bring a plate' events which would often end up in what we called a "Maningrida Circle." Guests would bring their own folding chairs and eskies and they'd invariably be placed in a large circle in the garden and we'd sit and talk the night away.

There was one party where I was told in clear terms that I was to supply a dessert. It was too late to buy a tub of ice cream so I managed to pilfer a

Roger and Trevor after a successful barramundi fishing trip at Berradja.

new box of art gum erasers from the school stores. These are cubes with one side stamped with the maker's logo. I sliced off the logos, rolled them in margarine and then desiccated coconut, and called them *crème caramel*. Come dessert time I listened to a few of the people who tried them.

"These are terrible," said Greg. "Don't tell Derek, he obviously tried hard."

One bloke threw his away, and then took another, convinced the first was stale.

No one else thought it was particularly funny, or even very clever, but I laughed so hard I had sore stomach muscles for days. It took years before my food was trusted again.

The first party I went to was in the first week after my arrival. It was run by Roger, a police sergeant with three boys at the school. The police houses were beside their station and we all met in the garden behind Roger's house, which backed onto the station yard. Looking over the fence I could see the lock up cells and one or two unhappy incarcerated faces peering out – miscreants in for the night.

This party was a good opportunity to meet a whole range of Balanda in the community who had nothing to do with the school. There were builders and plumbers, council workers, bank Johnnies, house wives and art centre workers. It was a good party with lots of laughter and joking about. At one point someone got handcuffed to the clothes line for about an hour because the keys were 'lost'.

I talked with Roger and Trevor Burke, one of my teacher colleagues, about fishing – a common topic of conversation in Maningrida, although I was the world's worst fisherman. I'd been a ranger, lived in Kakadu National Park on the river, and lived in Katherine, but had never managed to catch a barramundi on a line. I didn't need to when I was a ranger – tourists would usually catch their limit, which would be too much to eat, so I was always being given their excess. Barramundi are the most famous of the recreational fish in Australia's Top End, and people travel from across the world just to catch them. They put up a good fight, are good eating and some of them weigh 20 kg or more. They live in tidal rivers, mangrove forests and freshwater rivers and billabongs. Interestingly, they are all born males but they turn female when they get to be about 20 cm long, so all the big fish are female.

I had actually caught one once but no one ever believes me. I was fording a river in Kakadu National Park in a Land Cruiser ute. The water was deep, about bonnet height, and as I pushed through it I startled a small barramundi which leapt out of the water, sailed over the cab of the truck and landed in the tray. It was undersized, but I took him home anyway and ate him that night. Unfortunately that's the kind of story you need a number of witnesses to corroborate, and I was alone on that day. In the same river crossing another ranger reckoned he had hit a crocodile with his bull bar as he drove through. Nobody ever believed him either.

Anyway, Roger and Trevor took pity on me.

"Come out with us tomorrow," they invited. "We're going to Berraja Creek."

Trevor was the senior boys' and manual arts teacher when he worked at Maningrida. To me he seemed the right guy for the job. He was a tough looking bloke with close cropped hair and a big belly and he was immensely patient with a quiet controlled manner. He had worked for a while in Goulburn Jail, so his students didn't get up to much mischief and they all respected him highly. He was married to a nurse and had three beautiful daughters, his pride and joy, and two tiny little black dogs that looked like fluffy Chihuahuas. He and I made a peculiar sight whenever we walked anywhere together – two big blokes with the smallest dogs in town. He was also a mad keen fisherman.

Early the next morning a quick toot from his Hilux told me Trevor was ready to go. He had a twin cab ute and in the tray were his esky and a box of hand lines – strong fishing line coiled around plastic reels, nilsmaster lures, food and water for the day and an empty back pack.

"What's that for?" I asked.

"The fish."

"Yeah… right," I thought.

We picked up a few kids from the Cooper family's house in Top Camp. Their family owned a homeland centre named Gorrong-gorrong which was out the way we were heading so we dropped them off to stay with their grandfather, Willie Djolpa and his wife, Happy. Willie was the land owner of the creek we were heading to, so we promised him we'd drop some fish off on the way home. Roger had also brought the old man some loaves of bread fresh from the morning bakery in Maningrida.

It was wet season and the road became too wet to pass before we got anywhere near the creek so we had to park and walk in. Now I understood the back pack. We carried in our fishing gear, water and lunch and set out across a broad flood plain skirting a patch of tropical monsoon rain forest. Giant banyan fig trees stretched their arms 20 meters in all directions and every gap was filled with the crowns of Carpentaria palms, vines and bush apple trees. There was a large tamarind tree on the edge, a reminder of Maccassan trepang fishermen who visited this coast for more than 300 years from the Indonesian island of Macassar, now known as Sulawesi.

Pushing through the scrub we were hooked by a nasty little vine Trevor called *wait-a-while*, because it takes a few moments to unhook from your skin or clothing.

We reached the edge of a mangrove forest and entered its gloom. The mangroves there were small trees, perhaps four meters high, with masses of aerial roots that we had to clamber over. Luckily the mud was firm and we didn't sink to our knees like in other places. Deep in the forest we came to a small creek. The tide was out and the water was a meter down from the top of the bank. The creek was narrow enough for the trees on each side to meet in the middle so it was permanently shaded. A few dead trees could be seen sticking out of the shallow water, and mud skippers – small walking fish who can flick parts of their throats out like semaphore flags –skittered across the mud between conical shells known as *long bums*. These shells crawl slowly along the mud, or cling motionless to the mangrove roots. Small fiddler crabs came out from the holes and brandished their claws at each other like mad violinists. On the other bank I caught sight of a mangrove snake making his escape and in the distance we could hear blue herons and lots of unidentified little brown birds.

The creek was very pleasant and cool with no mosquitoes or sand flies, which was not what I had expected at all. That entire day was a bit odd in fact – an Indian summer fishing day, because I went there at other times and was driven mad by the insects.

Very soon we saw a small wall of water, known as a bore, move silently inland. The tide was returning.

Fishing here turned out to be just a matter of throwing a lure across the creek and pulling it back. We each chose a spot on the bank and I got my lure ready and played out about five meters of line. I may have never hooked a barramundi before but that didn't mean I was a complete slouch – I knew a bit about fishing.

I gathered enough line in my left hand and swung the lure towards a promising looking snag with my right and let the line play out. The lure sailed beautifully through the air - straight into the branches of a mangrove tree on the other side of the creek. Stuck! I pulled it this way and that but there was no way it was coming lose. My first cast and a $15 lure was lost! There was no way to get it back without risking becoming a crocodile's lunch by crossing the creek, and the tide was coming in fast. I cut the line.

By the time I'd tied on another lure, Roger had caught the first fish. It was on! My next cast was snatched as soon as it landed in the water and I pulled in a fine fish, my first barramundi. This wasn't sport - once they were hooked I was using nylon line with a twenty kilogram breaking strain, and I was confident that few fish would be able to break it. For a while it seemed every second cast was a success. Together we pulled in 23 large barramundi in just over an hour, and nine of them were mine! No one counted the small fish we threw back, but some of the large ones were real beauties, eight kilos or more of fighting fish.

We cooked one for lunch just outside the mangrove forest and ate heartily and drank a billy of tea. Trevor got out his back pack, which I admit I'd been a bit dubious about needing, and filled it with fish. We still had a dozen more that wouldn't fit, so we cut a stout pole and fed it past the gills and out the mouth of the big fish. On the return to the truck we took it in turns: two of us carried the pole and the third the back pack. We had more than a hundred kilos of fish.

Old Willie and Happy were as pleased as punch to receive some good sized fish to feed their family. We arrived home in style and spent a happy hour cleaning and filleting them over a few beers. It was a grand introduction to fishing the Maningrida way.

In the end I spent more time fishing in the sea than the rivers or creeks. My next door neighbour, Marie Matthews, was my inspiration here. Marie owned a half share of a four meter boat with another teacher, and she was as expert at fishing as she was in cooking her famous vanilla slices, known to everyone in town as *snot blocks*.

Marie was a nun, a Sister of Mercy from a convent in Newcastle. Her calling for the church was teaching and she worked at Maningrida CEC for many years before her retirement, after which she returned to the convent. She was just under 60 years old when I moved in next door. An excellent and committed teacher, she taught a mixed age class for kids who spoke a high level of English. Several generations of primary students went through her classes; many were with her for three or four years.

We used to go fishing out to sea for the whole day, leaving before dawn and returning just after dark. Marie would usually have two or three passengers every weekend and when I could go I'd drive her Hilux down to the barge landing and back the trailer into the sea. Marie would unwind the cable and float the boat, and then stand in the water holding it until I'd parked the car. Climbing in, in a maneuver she always called *getting her leg over*, Sister Marie would take control as captain of her little ship. We'd set off, her other guests and me lounging on the bow or sitting on the esky, whilst she drove.

There are two islands off the mouth of the Liverpool River. The closest and biggest is Entrance Island, which has a sheltered beach and a few shade trees, so it was here we used to stop for 'dinner camp'. The second is Haul Round Island, which we always imaginatively called 'Second Island'. It is really just a series of rocky reefs which have collected enough sand and vegetation to rate a lighthouse. Haul Round Island is about 12 kilometers from the coast and is an important breeding site for roseate and bridled terns and other sea birds, and sometimes turtles come up and lay their eggs in the sand. The reefs around this area are good for catching coral trout and trevally and, on occasion, if we had a chance to go snorkeling when the weather and tide were right, we'd catch blue lobsters called *painted crays*.

There was another rocky reef system we'd head out to a couple of kilometers east of Entrance Island, as it was usually very productive. It only ever appeared at low tide and we'd motor around the rocks trailing a couple of lures called *spoons.* They have a single large hook and a semi-flat piece of shiny metal that flashes in the sun and sends the fish crazy. Spoons usually attract a number of great fighting fish like skinnies (queenfish) and golden trevally, but also coral trout, Spanish mackerel and sometimes tuna take them.

The first time I was out at this reef with Marie I was holding a hand line with a good thick nylon string that meant there was little chance of it breaking unless I caught a whale. I threw the lure out as Marie instructed and let out about 50 meters of line then sat back to wait, not knowing really what to expect. After ten minutes of motoring along, lulled by the rocking of the boat and the engine noise, I was day dreaming. All of a sudden a fish struck the lure, hard. The line went wild and I had to let a few winds off to stop being pulled into the water. It whipped around and around the hand reel and each time whacked against my forearm, leaving livid welts

"Got one" I yelled. Marie stopped the engine and Peter, who had the other line out, quickly started to wind his in hoping to get a fish also. I started to wind in and managed three or four loops around the reel before the fish was fighting again. Wow, it was strong! Having never used a rod and reel for this sort of fishing I can't comment on that, but even with a hand line it's exciting.

The fish came closer as I wound it in and at one point it leapt out of the water.

"Skinny, a big one," Marie identified.

As it came close to the boat Peter picked up a wicked looking hook called a gaff. When the fish was in reach he speared it with a quick swipe upwards and lifted it into the boat, where it flapped madly on the floor. It was massive, about a meter long, and when we put it into an old canvas mail bag it left about 20 centimeters of its tail still sticking out.

Beautifully streamlined and consummate predators, skinnies are fast and ruthless. They are scaleless with smooth silver, white and yellow skin and large eyes. Their bodies are thin, only a few centimeters thick, but a big one can be 20 centimeters tall and over a meter long.

We caught maybe 15 more that first trip and about a dozen of them went into the canvas bag. Then we went to Entrance Island for a picnic. The pattern, I was to learn, was always the same. We'd arrive there mid-morning and anchor the boat and be joined by another boat load or two of people. We'd set out and collect firewood, light the fire, boil the billy, then cook a fish in the coals of the fire. We'd eat our fill of delicious fresh fish, then complete the meal with Marie's chocolate cake and drink more tea. People who were really keen would go fishing again with Marie; the rest would lounge in the shade and read or sleep for a few hours, or throw a line in off the beach.

Heading home during the magnificent Top End sunset we were back in Maningrida at last light with time to tow the boat around and share the fish out to families we knew, then wash the boat and clean the fish we had kept.

At school the next week, a Monday morning ritual occurred with teachers who had been fishing over the weekend comparing the welt marks made by the fishing lines. Getting a good whipping meant a good day's fishing.

Marie used to go up river for barramundi, but that was a hard day's work for me – there was a lot of time between fish, mosquitoes as big as hummingbirds and nowhere to land and picnic. Plus she always used a light fishing line and a rod because it was more 'sporting'. They were trips for the experts and I rarely rated being allowed to go. The best I saw Marie do was bring home a barramundi one day that was so big she could have put her head in its mouth. Not bad for a little old lady.

One day I went out to Entrance Island to fish with Marie and two visitors, who were also nuns. All day I tried thinking of jokes about three nuns in a boat, but the best joke was written by one of the nuns herself. After I'd lit a cooking fire on the island one of the sisters made a billy of tea with water she'd taken straight from the sea. Her god ignored her that day; the tea was terrible, but we all had a good laugh.

10
JAPI

Dry season in Arnhem Land brings in the ceremony season that can last right up to the next wet season, when the roads get once again cut by the rising rivers and floodplains. There are a number of ceremonies that can last several months and involve special camps in the bush, sometimes with roads being closed and everyone on tenterhooks in case they break some rule or other.

The *japi* or young men's initiation ceremonies are different. They are celebrations and public events and the time when boys become men. There's a sense of excitement in the air as the time comes close, tempered by a little wide eyed fear of the initiates.

In November the rains are eagerly awaited. Everywhere the bush is tinder dry and ready to burn for anyone with time to light a match. The air is heavy with humidity, the days are stinking hot and great thunderclouds flash at night on the horizon to tease and taunt anyone sweltering under their mosquito nets, promising rain but rarely delivering.

Japi initiation: the singing reaches a crescendo and the dancers become more frenetic as the circumcision is done.

Usually the last opportunity for ceremonies before the floods is November and right across Arnhem Land parents ask everyone in their extended community to help get their boys initiated.

At Yilan I arrived one Monday for a regular week's teaching just before 8 am. I'd left home at first light and the road had been easy, without any delays, so the 110 kilometers had taken just over three hours. The head man of the community was Kevin Jarwugurr, a big man in his early fifties. His wife, Dawn Yaramalanga, worked as teacher with another woman named Bonny Burangarra and there were generally about ten kids attending the school from three or four families. Kevin and Dawn owned a recently finished mud brick house which had two rooms with a breezeway between them, and wide verandahs. The other families lived outside when the weather was good but in the wet season they'd build shelters using rough cut bush poles and corrugated iron.

Because it was so hot everyone, including Kevin and his family, slept outside under large rectangular mosquito nets with a green striped cloth roof. These were known far and wide as *Maningrida* nets, as if that's some sort of statement about conditions in the community.

Yilan's school building was a square metal construction like those at Marrkolidjban and Ji-marda. It had a great shade tree beside it - a giant woollybutt (*Eucalyptus miniata*), which usually caught the breeze from the beach a couple of hundred meters away across the dunes. It was a very pleasant place to stay in the dry season.

In the wet season the only way to get to Yilan was to walk in about three kilometers from Ji-marda, through clouds of mosquitoes among stands of bush apple trees, then wade through a reed swamp and clamber through a small mangrove forest. I carried a backpack of school supplies and my swag and Turkey trotted along the track beside me, or swam through the deepest parts where the track was flooded. When it was sunny the sand on the track would get so hot in the middle of the day that Turkey learned to follow the thin strip of vegetation down the centre of the road to avoid burning his feet.

There's a legend told around the camp about a previous visiting teacher who was unwilling to walk through the swamp and hit on a method of delivering supplies to the school from the air. Apparently she'd fly low over the school in a Cessna and drop boxes of pencils and exercise books out the door, wave cheerily then head off back to Maningrida.

The swamp usually dried out enough to drive through by the beginning of May so getting there was much easier in the school vehicle and life was much more comfortable. I could take an esky and fresh food, and my swag – a foam mattress rolled up in canvas with a large comfy pillow and a light blanket. The canvas could fold out on each side of the mattress to form a large ground sheet, or it could be folded back across the bed to act as a wind break in the cold, or even protect you from light rain. Swags are funny things. People who use them a lot fall in love with them like musicians fall in love with their instruments. I suppose it's only fitting, when you spend a third of your day with something you're bound to either love it or loath it.

Kevin came over from his house to meet me when I parked beside the school.

"*Japi* coming," he said. "Big mob of people. All that Kunwinjku mob and Djinang mob will dance."

"Japi? Whose japi?" I asked.

"Wilton, Leon, Ian and Clint, plus two fellas from Milingimbi."

Wilton Ali was Kevin and Dawn's son, a polite and quiet lad of 13 years who attended the school regularly. He was a great kid, and really one of the mainstays of Yilan School, but he also spent time in Maningrida so I'd known him for quite a while. I knew the others from Maningrida but I didn't know the Milingimbi boys - their families were bringing them from their homelands serviced by Milingimbi. With six initiates this japi was going to be a big and expensive affair. I had heard that more often only two or three boys were involved but this late in the year perhaps there was a sense of urgency.

We ran school as normal. Wilton and the other boys even attended, seemingly unconcerned about what was about to happen. Around lunch time Land Cruiser utes began to arrive with lots of "yakaiing" and excitement. Some carried more than twenty people. Trucks came in from Maningrida, Garmardi and Wurdeja and the two boys from Ramingining arrive with their families and a load of other hangers on. The Mumeka mob arrived later, and behind them in a school troop carrier drove Murray Garde.

"I didn't expect to see you here," I said as he came into the school.

"I would have been alone at Mumeka," he replied. "Everyone is here." It was true. Murray himself had driven most of the kids from Mumeka School in his troop carrier. I was glad he was there. As an old hand in homeland centers he had been to a number of these ceremonies and I thought he'd be able to answer a lot of my questions about what was happening.

"Tonight they'll paint the boys up in ochre and there'll be a lot of singing. Same thing tomorrow. A *japi* usually lasts about three days. On the last morning the boys are circumcised then taken off into the bush for some seclusion."

The Kunwinjku men from Mumeka had been 'employed' to do the dancing and singing for the ceremony, as they often were. They were the best song men and with their characteristic 'stomp' dancing they were in demand across the region. They'd often travel hundreds of kilometers, and groups had also travelled to Japan and Germany to perform. At Yilan, they were to be paid in presents. A growing pile of blankets, 'slabs' of flour about the same size and shape as bags of cement, new bed sheets, tinned food, some clothing and packets of cigarettes, tea and sugar, started to appear outside Kevin's house. Most of the Burarra people brought a contribution. I felt chagrined that I'd brought nothing, but I figured I could pay my way by taking photographs and giving people copies afterwards. Murray, who was in the know, had brought a slab of flour.

Because the school had the best shade tree and Murray was in there anyway, the Mumeka guys set up their camp around us. That didn't take long. Someone lit a fire for a billy and someone else unfolded a blue tarp I'd had in the school store room. They'd brought little with them. Many people drifted off towards the beach and a few blokes left in Land Cruisers with their shot guns to look for wallabies. Dawn and the other ladies from Yilan had spent the day making dampers and there was plenty to go round. Her dampers were disks of bread, about the size of a frisbee, made from flour and water and baked in the hot coals of their fires. People would eat them by brushing off the ash from the crust and just breaking a piece off. Dampers are filling and delicious, if not exactly nutritious, especially when still hot. There were a few squeeze bottles of honey around which made them really tasty.

By late afternoon the Mumeka musicians started practising and the sounds of the song men with their clap sticks and the didgeridoo drifted across the community.

The didgeridoo is the most famous of all Australian instruments. People often think it is synonymous with all Aboriginal tribes but that is not so - only the tribes of the tropical north ever used it. Southern groups traditionally had clap sticks – short hardwood sticks, sometimes painted, often not, or they used two boomerangs to clap out a beat - but they never copied or invented a didge of their own.

One reason didgeridoos were limited to the tropical north and never spread across the country is that the hollow wood is made by termites that eat out the trunk and branches of eucalyptus trees like the stringybark tree. I went out once with Old Michael, the wood carver, and a few of the kids from Gamardi to get some timber to make some. We walked through the bush and every now and then Old Michael would stop next to a tree and tap it with his fingernail. He'd listen for a hollow sound.

"This one, him no good, *nyika gun-molamola*," he would say or, "This one, *gun-molamola*, him good."

I tapped every tree I passed but could hear no

difference. I tried the trees Old Michael had said were hollow and they still sounded the same. Eventually Old Michael chose three trees with a diameter of about 20 centimeters and we chopped them down with axes. He was right each time. As they fell we could see the entire tree had been hollowed out by termites and there was nothing left in the middle apart from tissue-thin dark brown wood pulp structures the termites had constructed that reminded me of the sinus bones you see in the skulls of long dead animals.

We cut each tree trunk into lengths of about two meters and stripped off the bark before carrying them back to Gamardi. Old Michael had a saw in his camp and he quickly squared off the ends of each log and then we sat down with small axes and carved off the green outer wood. This thinned the didgeridoos to about ten centimeters. The pulp in the inside fell out after a few sharp bangs with the back of the axe and a bit of shaking.

To finish them the didgeridoos are often painted. Those made for sale in the art shops can be extraordinary objects of art with traditional designs of patterns or even X-ray style paintings down their length. With no pretentions of design myself, I painted mine brown with a mixture of PVA glue and the red ochre the kids ground up for me and put two bands of white around the business end. The mouth end is often padded with beeswax to make it more comfortable to blow or to narrow the tube but I never went that far with it.

Didgeridoos are keyed the same way you can tune a trombone – by varying the length. The experts will cut sections off to key them to C, or A minor. I have got no idea what key mine is but I was pretty pleased with it when I'd finished.

To play them you purse your lips and create a vibration down the tube by blowing. Varying the amount of air and the tightness or angle of your lips changes the sound and throwing in your voice in a rhythmic fashion can make some really interesting music. Good players can play nonstop for ages. They develop a circular breathing technique where they continually blow to make the sound but can also inhale at the same time, getting their cheeks to work like the bags of bagpipes in the meantime. They can also get this hooting sound, like a fog horn, during their playing which I was never able to master.

In Yilan for the *japi* one of the didgeridoo players was Owen Yalandja and the lead singers were two small men named Kevin Djimarr and Jimmy Djarrbbarali. These were the same guys I saw recorded at Mumeka for a music CD a few years later. Kevin spent the week painted entirely in white ochre like a ghost.

The japi and other businesses in Arnhem Land were called *corroborees* by the first Balanda who write about the area. But I never heard that word used by the Arnhem Landers. To them, and us, they were *business*. There was *sorry business* when someone had died and funerals could last a week or two. The Morning Star ceremony was business, and the infamous but secret *gunapipi*, which could last six months, was really serious business and, incidentally, about the only indigenous ceremony in Australia which uses drums. This time we were attending the japi, or *young man's business*.

Time has changed the use of other words too. To Kyle-Little 50 years ago, the men, even proud warriors, were always "boys" and to Mountford and Simpson the children were called *pikininies* and the women *lubras* or *gins*. These words aren't really used around Maningrida any more, if they ever really were, and even to read them feels odd and disrespectful.

Owen had incredible skill with the didgeridoo. He would sit still on the ground with one foot extended and place the end of the didgeridoo between his toes to steady it. Then, apparently without effort, the drone would start and the didge would sing. He would tap rhythm on the side of the didge with his finger nails and the drone would turn into a beat, with occasional fog horn sounds erupting through the music. Kevin and others would start the clap sticks and sing short bursts of song over and over again.

In the early evening the stage was set. The circular 'stomping ground' had been cleared of all rubbish and vegetation for the dancing. The musicians sat on blue tarps on one side and the boys, who had disappeared for most of the afternoon, were brought, their legs, arms and heads red from ochre and their faces decorated with lines of white clay like some exotic living peace sign. They were led by the dancers to the tarps and sat quietly together at the edge of the circular stomping ground near the musicians, with their heads bowed. They had no part to play other than to watch.

In the distance men shouted and hissed what sounded like a team chant:

Tss... tsss... tsss... ARRRR... HOI!!

Then, in single file they danced over to the stage and gathered round. The dance continued in a circular fashion, anticlockwise. The men and even very young boys were all painted white or red with ochre and wearing bright red cloths called nargas around their waists. They stomped their feet hard into the sand to the beat of the music, plumes of dust rising above. Like a beacon the ochred white skin of Murray stood out among them but he seamlessly fit into the dance as if he'd grown up with it. I could feel the vibrations through the ground. Every few seconds they'd shout and some would run to the centre of the circle and stomp in a show of energy to the shouts of everyone,

Tss... tsss... tsss... ARRRR... HOI!

On the final *hoi* there'd be a pause in the music and people would freeze for a second in a dramatic pose. Then it would start again. I tried dancing like this once or twice in later years but, Luddite that I am, I could never get the right beat. They'd have their final *hoi* for the stanza and freeze, and then half a second later a lone *hoi* from me would sail across the silent crowd, leaving me feeling like a clumsy idiot.

While the men did their stomp dancing the women and girls danced in as well. They came in shuffling and skirted round the stage area in a single file, heads bowed, swinging their white clay painted arms from left to right with the music and twisting one foot side to side in the sand. It was a simple dance compared to the athletic stomping of the men that even I thought I could accomplish if I was ever asked to pretend to be a woman.

I was sitting next to Alan Cooper, a Burarra man from Ji-malawa, which lies only about 15 kilometers south of Yilan. He had connections with the Djinang mob from Gamardi, and said that tomorrow they would be dancing too.

"You will dance with us," he said simply.

"Hmm, maybe," I said, as if I'd have a choice. My dancing skills in any situation are reminiscent of Mr Bean.

"Do you dance like this?" I asked.

"No, different one, you'll see."

Suddenly a woman rushed forward through the crowd and speared me!

"What...?" I exclaimed. I'd been hit with a short spear with a ball of paperbark tied to the end. Margaret Rinbuma from Gamardi, painted white, her hair wild with grass pushed through it, was causing trouble. She was going through the crowd spearing people and throwing cigarettes at them. Alan said that was her role, to cause mischief.

"She's proper cheeky," he laughed.

I looked around. The crowd had grown to about 200 people and here and there were several crazy women, attacking people with padded spears or hitting them with branches. There was a great deal of laughter. Sometimes someone would make a break for it and run into the darkness, and the women would follow a short way to everyone's cheering.

The show went on until well after dark, and finally

broke up for the evening at about 9 o'clock. Back at the school I unrolled my swag on the ground near the fire and lay on the mattress with the canvas stretching out as a ground sheet. I had a small tape recorder and a couple of blank cassettes which the Kunwinjku men wanted to borrow so they could hear themselves singing and playing. Soon 20 men were sitting around the fire singing, with clap sticks and the didgeridoo. Wilton and Leon were there sitting on my canvas and I chatted to them about what was going to happen. Wilton admitted to being nervous, but was really proud that at last he was to become a man.

The music went on for hours - I know because they'd filled both 90 minute cassette tapes by the morning, but, despite the noise and the movement of people around me, I quickly fell asleep and missed the lot. I woke up at dawn with Wilton, Leon and one or two other blokes I didn't know all sharing my canvas.

The second morning was surprisingly normal. Murray and I ran the school in the morning with both Yilan and Mumeka kids attending, plus anyone else who happened to be around. We went fishing on the beach in the afternoon because the tide was in. At low tide the water could be a kilometer away across sandy flats, which is a good time to find crabs in their holes, but pretty poor fishing. One boy, caught a small black tipped reef shark and was 'bitten'- somehow cutting his finger on the shark's teeth as he took the hook out of its mouth. I helped him with first aid but Kevin took over with some bush medicine. He collected leaves from the purple flowered dune vine he called *gongorra* and baked them quickly over hot coals, and then he wrapped the boy's wound up with them. The gongorra leaves are known to have antiseptic properties and coastal people have used them as medicine for centuries. It was an incident that was to inspire a chapter in the novel *Tammy Damulkurra* I wrote with students a few years later.

In the afternoon Alan came and got me to get ready for our dance. Still dubious I followed him to where the Gamardi men were painting up. Most were using white ochre but there was red ochre there too. I was given a red cloth nagar and I took off my shirt for the ochre. I chose the red ochre thinking it might make me blend in a little more, though there was fat chance of that – I am two meters tall, and towered over the rest of them.

I still hadn't been told what to do, but Alan did say we were doing the "peewee dance". A peewee is a small black and white bird, like a tiny magpie. OK, I thought, I can be a tiny magpie.

I went with the men to the dancing ground. A didgeridoo began to drone, the song men sang and the guys started to dance around the circle. I followed them, doing everything they were doing a second or two later. At regular intervals we would rush to the centre of the circle, drop to our haunches and jump around a bit in a squat, making bird noises:

Pirrwt, pirrwt, and up and around we went again. *Pirrwt, pirrwt.*

I was using muscles I'd never used before. My thighs were sore for days afterwards.

Pirrwt, pirrwt. We danced like this for hours. Well, a few minutes at least. It was torture – an athleticism

I wasn't designed for, but the Gamardi blokes didn't have any problems. Then it was over and I could go and sit for the rest of the evening and watch.

I was talking later to Alan and said, yes, I had enjoyed dancing… "but I wasn't very good at it."

"Yo-ai," he agreed, looking me in the eye, "you are not a good dancer."

The Gamardi people danced again later that evening and the next one too. I saw them dance a number of times at other ceremonies and they clearly had a great time performing, but strangely, though nobody said anything, I was never asked to dance with them ever again.

The second night was similar in terms of dance and singing but the boys were painted differently. Four of the boys had had their entire bodies reddened with ochre and starting on their upper thighs and moving up across their bellies and chests in brilliant white clay were two long yam vines, crossing each other under their necks. Long 'socks' of a light yellow brown clay stretched to above their knees and arm tassels of coloured wool or strings of feathers hung from their upper arms. Their reddened faces were lined with white clay. The designs on Clint's belly differed slightly from the others in that he also had the white figure of a man standing among the vines.

Ian Carter and one of the boys from Milingimbi were painted very differently, perhaps because of their connections with the Yolngu tribes further east. I had watched the artist carefully wrap a bed sheet around each boy. Then, as someone held the sheet tight against their neck, he took a mouthful of wet ochre paint and blew it out straight into the boy's face. A fine spray of white ochre covered their skin and hair, transforming them so only their dark eyes showed any colour. When the sheet was dropped other men tied bracelets of orange parrot feathers around their upper arms and a sacred dilly bag, whose contents I never discovered, was tied around their neck.

At last, again ready for the show, the boys were led by the Kunwinjku stomp dancers back to their positions beside the stomping ground.

Two nights of excitement, dance and song, with a few hours each morning running school for anyone who turned up for the distraction, passed quickly. On the third afternoon the mood changed. The men were up and out in the bush with the boys. I could hear them talking and went over to investigate. The initiates had been daubed in red and white ochre most of the week, but this time they were *really* being painted. The boys were living works of art. They looked from a distance to be wearing singlets with geometric designs across their bellies and vertical lines running up to their shoulders like straps. Each design was filled with intricately cross hatched *rarrk*. Their arms were reddened with ochre and their faces darkened with coals, except for white clay lines across their foreheads. Wilton had skeins of coloured wool hanging from each arm. Leon had strings of white and orange parrot feathers. Both wore new cloth *nagas* of brightly patterned material.

Rarrk is the style of painting I'd seen many times on bark paintings. The artist forms an image using hundreds of narrow lines and hatch work. It is labour intensive indeed, and the boys had had to lie motionless for hours whilst the artists did their work. They hadn't eaten or had much sleep, but the next morning was the big day, the culmination of the whole business. I watched as Wilton stood up. He had become a living masterpiece and was ready. His father Kevin and other relatives asked me to take a photograph. They posed, like a proud family at any coming-of-age ceremony or a college graduation, a big smile on the men's lips, a slight worried look on Wilton's painted face.

The dancing and singing started again. Nearly 300 people had come from all directions and gathered to celebrate. It was for them the end of boyhood and the beginning of manhood, a rite of passage their forefathers had gone through for centuries and I felt privileged to be a witness.

By the time I climbed out of my swag just after dawn the next morning I saw that the dance ground had been transformed. In the centre a couple of mattresses had been walled by bed sheets. This was to be the site of the circumcision and the cloth walls gave privacy from prying eyes. I stood back respectfully, hesitating on the edge or the dance ground but Jimmy Gularawuna was there and he took me under his wing.

There was the sound of clap sticks and a didgeridoo then a shout from the scrub and a massed *Tss... tsss... tsss... ARRRR...*

The initiates were on their way.

The boys were carried on the shoulders of uncles,

hunched over, looking down and hooded by cloth sheets. Around them the Kunwinjku stomp dances jumped and cavorted about. The procession was noisy, dusty and very, very impressive. Nothing in my own upbringing and growth into a man had been anything like this. I watched with awe.

Jimmy Gularawuna grabbed my arm. My plans of standing respectfully back were forgotten. He pulled me into the circle to stand right at the edge of the walled mattresses.

The dancers arrived and started to circle the ground, a great mob of shouting, hissing stomping men going round and round. The women were in single file, singing out at the tops of their voices, dancing in a larger circle around the men.

Tss... tsss... tsss... ARRRR.

A couple of men had climbed into the walled area. One was an old, old man - the medicine man. I hadn't noticed him before, but he was the only one there with no ochre painted on him. Jimmy said he was the "doctor". He was very old, with snow white hair and rail thin arms with loose sagging grey skin. His hands shook and he panted from the effort of stepping over the cloth wall.

In time the boys were brought in too. Their uncles lay down on the mattresses and they were made to lie on top of them. The uncles were then able to put their arms around the boys' chests and clamp them tightly. The Kunwinjku, with Murray among them, continued dancing the circle, singing, shouting and stomping. The atmosphere was electric.

I watched as the doddering old 'doctor' took out

a razor blade. Wilton's nagar was removed and the old man pinched his foreskin between the fingers of his left hand and, without any further ceremony, sawed it off with the razor blade. Wow! Wilton bit down hard on the dilly bag that'd been placed in his mouth, but he never moved or made a sound. I cringed at the thought of the pain and my respect for his bravery was unbounded. The doctor checked his work. Oh no! There was more to cut off. He moved in again with the razor blade and I saw him slice off more skin.

Tss... tsss... tsss... ARRRR.

The dancers were frenetic. Their dancing and their noise continued as the doctor moved on to the next boy. I had tears in my eyes. Again, the boy's stoic bravery was impressive. When each boy was done the uncles picked up them up and carried them off into the scrub. Wilton's head lolled like he had fainted. In a bush camp their wounds were to be treated by antiseptic leaves. The old man put the foreskins into his pocket and tottered off to do whatever he had to do with them. I never saw him again.

Jimmy Gularawuna told me that one of the rules for the boys now would be to not touch food until the wounds healed. They would be fed by another man using chop sticks and they couldn't speak to any women.

Later, I was sitting in the shade talking with Ian's family: my neighbours in Maningrida. Sabrina, a beautiful girl of about 15 who called me her "big son" because in kin relationships terms she was my mother, was talking about culture.

"You know, Derek," she said, "You Balanda mob have got no culture."

I was immediately defensive. "Of course we do," I replied. Then, getting flustered, I tried to think of anything that would compete on a cultural level from my own background with what I'd just seen. Culture is an interesting concept and hard to define. I was on the spot and I am not proud of my answer:

"Of course we do, we have, umm... well... yes, we have the Easter Bunny and Santa Claus!"

11

THE SUNSHINE GIRLS and TAMMY DAMULKURRA

I became the senior teacher of the secondary section of Maningrida Community Education Centre in 1994. This meant giving up the peripatetic lifestyle I'd enjoyed as a visiting teacher and focusing on the classes that made up the high school. There were three classes – Eagle Class, Tiger Class and Kangaroo Class, for about 90 kids on the roll. They were more or less streamed, along the lines of the attendance history of the kids and their English literacy levels. Kangaroo class was for kids who needed to work on their literacy and numeracy to get into the higher level courses. They were often from more mobile families who would come and go from Maningrida, or from families who valued school little and came rarely. For them there were always a hundred reasons to stay home.

We taught certificated curriculum programs developed in the Northern Territory, called Foundation Studies and General Studies. The Foundation Studies program was meant to be a preparation for students to get into and handle the rigours of the General Studies program, which was a legitimate secondary school level course. In 1994 there were yet to be graduates of this course anywhere in the Territory.

I took on teaching the General Studies class. They ranged in age from 13 years to 18 years old. Most of them were girls and most were Burarra, but there were some from Beswick, Milingimbi and other areas. They were a strong class and early on we did a trip to Darwin and they all earned their *AustSwim* bronze medallion and participated in outdoor education programs like snorkeling, archery, rock climbing and canoeing.

After a while I started to notice odd behaviour in the class. The young men (never 'boys', once they were initiated) would sit on one side of the room and the girls the other. Nothing unusual about that in any school, but here the young men also started to avoid looking across at the girls and some would even sit at their desk holding their hand up to the side of their face to avoid seeing them accidentally. When they spoke, if they ever did, it was in whispers. This was never anything they were willing to talk about with me.

I spoke to some of the Aboriginal members of the school staff as it was clear there was a problem. Traditionally, different skin groups have avoidance relationships. We obviously had some very uncomfortable interrelationships at play in the class, which were getting worse as the students were getting older. It was imperative we did something about it, and quickly, because the guys would have soon voted with their feet and disappeared from school forever.

The answer was simple in the end. Eagle Class became a girls' class studying General Studies, Tiger Class became all the young men and they studied Foundation Studies, except for one or two General Studies guys who kept going on the higher course at their own pace. Kangaroo Class became a bit of a mix of irregular attenders, and younger girls and boys who were not yet initiated.

Suddenly I was the teacher for a group of 15 opinionated, strong, beautiful young women. They were undoubtedly the most highly literate group of girls the community had ever seen. They were the crème de la crème. At least that's what I told them and their egos blossomed. Self esteem building has always been part of my teaching programs and these girls grabbed whatever was offered with both hands. Very soon, Sabrina (the same girl who was at the Japi at Yilan) and a couple of other girls came and saw me.

"We don't want to be Eagle Class any more, *my Big Son*, we want to be *The Sunshine Girls*, she said.

"Ngaw, yes," the others agreed. On the face of it, it seemed a good idea. The girls were getting a group identity and allowing it to evolve. They were becoming a team. In the end they became *The Sunshine Girls of Eagle Class* and their power soared. Little kids, including little boys, would whisper to each other:

"I want to be a Sunshine Girl when I grow up."

One afternoon I filmed them gathered in a group, the beach behind them and flowers in their hair.

"Hi there," they said a hundred times in practice. "We are the Sunshine Girls from Maningrida, and you're watching *Imparja TV*!"

I sent the final tape to Imparja Television in Alice Springs and yes, they played it, at least every day for months between programs or during ad breaks. The girls were ten feet tall.

In hindsight this ego building was all very well for the Sunshine Girls, but for the other girls in Kangaroo Class it was a bit unfair. They were irregular attenders and less academic anyway, and as the Sunshine Girls shone brighter, the others were more and more shaded. It was a shame and if I had my time again… well, easier said than done.

I taught the Sunshine Girls for 18 months and we had a great time. They worked hard and several of them graduated with the General Studies Certificate of Education - the first graduates the Northern Territory had seen. The whole community was proud of them. One of the girls, Jacqueline Phillips, did so well that when she applied for an exchange scholarship to the USA she was accepted. She was the first Indigenous girl to exchange on this program and she lived for 12 months in Connecticut with an African American family. I was very proud of her. Jacqui was in grade 2 in my first class in Maningrida back in 1989, so I had known her for a long time.

Teaching English literature to Aboriginal kids has always been a challenge on several levels, one of which was that most of the literature out there had little to interest them. There were no novels, for example, which dealt with Indigenous teenagers like themselves or their issues. I was on my October holidays lying on a beach somewhere wondering how to deal with this problem and suddenly had a brain wave.

I know, I thought. If there's no book out there they want to read, we'll have to write our own.

That was the birth of *Tammy Damulkurra*.

The first day back at school I put up a large piece of butcher's paper on the wall, handed out some new exercise books and said to the class, with what I hoped was unbridled infectious enthusiasm:

"Right! Pens out, we're going to do some creative writing."

I could sense a feeling of general resignation as a *what's-he-going-to-make-us-do-now?* expression appeared on the girls' faces. More than a few rolled their eyes and sighed. They'd seen me like this before.

"Story time, let's write. First we need a character. What will his name be?"

"His?" No way was the main character ever going to be about a male. These were the Sunshine Girls I was teaching! We needed a girl's name.

"Justina...? Jacqui...?" I asked all the girls. Could we use one of their names? "No, shame job!" was the answer. About then we had a visit from an ex-student, Tammy Birch.

"Hi Tammy, we're going to write about a girl in a story, can we use your name?"

"No worries," she replied.

For a second name we used 'Eagle' because we were Eagle Class: 'Tammy Eagle'. But, we thought, that made her sound more like a Cherokee. Eagle in Burarra is Damulkurra. We had her name.

I wrote 'Tammy Damulkurra' on the centre of the butcher's paper and drew a line from her name to a corner and wrote 'family', another line to 'What does she like and do?', and a third to 'Where does she live?' The girls were getting involved. Soon we had lists of family members, her hobbies, a boyfriend, and some details about her house in Top Camp and loads of other information.

I took the paper home that night and prepared a worksheet. I just wrote a first paragraph or two and then asked questions.

> *Tammy woke and stretched herself lazily on her foam mattress. She lay for a while before standing up quietly so as not to wake her sister, who was curled into a small ball under the sheet. The old lady, her grandmother, snored softly on the mattress by the windows.*
> *What happened next?*
> *Where did she go?*
> *Who else was there?*

The next day the girls took the worksheet and started, reluctantly, to write. They answered the questions with any ideas in a couple of words. Then we shared them and together decided which ones were best and where the story would go. I went home that evening and wrote up what we'd decided, so we had another section to write the next day. This became a pattern, and to say they were excited by the project by the end would be an understatement. Justina

Williams, for example, and I know because I kept her exercise book, went from struggling to write six lines on the first day to at least two pages of tightly written narrative every day a couple of weeks later.

By the third week we had three chapters finished. I reckoned it was pretty good and someone suggested we should publish it. It became the story of 15 year old Tammy, who lived in Maningrida, but had a fight with another girl who was seen talking with Tammy's boyfriend. She was sent by her angry parents to stay at their outstation, Gochilawa, which we based on Yilan Outstation (*Gochilawa* means horizon, like the line you see on the beach at low tide at Yilan when the sea is kilometers away). Tammy and her brother go hunting and fishing and listen to old folks tell stories until her brother gets bitten by a shark. They come back to Maningrida. Tammy is now a 'single' and when she's offered a place at a boarding school in Darwin she takes it. And there, of course, she catches the eye of a new boy and knows everything is going to be all right.

In Canberra, Aboriginal Studies Press (ASP) publishes non-fiction titles about Indigenous topics. I wondered if they'd be interested in a novel written by Aboriginal teenagers and their teacher from Maningrida, so I posted them a copy of the first three chapters. The novel, which is only 15,000 words, took us six weeks to finish, but within days ASP called and said they'd love to publish it, and asked if we could send the complete book!

It moved fast from there. I found an illustrator, a young woman named Celia Adams, who did a dozen black and white illustrations for the beginning of the chapters. I wanted the girls to receive any royalties the book might earn, rather than the Department of Education, which strictly speaking was entitled to them. I asked the boss to give me permission to change the rules a bit and the girls had to sign an agreement with me as the major author, as ASP could only deal with one author. A few royalties came in over the first few years and I used to distribute them out to the girls when I visited Maningrida. It was a great way to keep in contact with them but no one ever got rich.

There were a few complications. The book contained two Dreamtime stories which were written by two of the girls as part of an earlier program they'd done. These however were traditional stories *owned* by senior men in their families, so we had to get them to sign intellectual property releases.

It took 12 months for the book to be published. I had moved to Pularumpi by the next July so had to fly in for the launch but I was in the school office when a call came through from the publishers:

"Can we organize a radio interview over the phone with some of the girls?"

"Sure," I said. "That's great news."

The girls decided Jackie Phillips had the best English and that she should do the interview, so at the appointed time we all crowded into the Principal's office to use the phone. The interview started right on time:

"And today we're talking with Jackie Phillips from Maningrida. Jackie is one of the authors of a new novel written for Aboriginal teenagers *by* Aboriginal teenagers, named *Tammy Damulkurra*. Congratulations, Jackie, how does it feel? You're a published author."

"Good."

"I hear it took six weeks to write the book. Was it fun? Did you like it?"

Long pause.

"Yes."

"There were about ten other girls weren't there...?"

"Um, yes."

(I whispered: "Come on, Jackie, this is radio, say something.")

"Can you tell us a little about the story?"

Long pause.

"Um... I forget."

"It's a love story about a teenage girl in Maningrida isn't it? She goes to a disco and gets in a fight doesn't she?"

"....yes."

The interview went on but the usually verbose teenager, who could be hard to shut up on occasion, was now monosyllabic. As a radio interview I think no one would call it a must-listen runaway success.

The book launch turned out to be a big community event hosted by the Maningrida Shop. Dale Gordes, the manager, had even organized bright yellow T-shirts with the front cover of the book printed across the chest. We had a book signing on the shop veranda with plates of cheese and biscuits. The girls sat in a line along trestle tables wearing their T-shirts and passed fresh books from a pile on the left to each other one at a time, signing them as they passed. That afternoon we sold 100 copies of *Tammy Damulkurra*, and had our 15 minutes of fame.

The local member, Maurice Rioli, flew in from Darwin to officially launch the book. He later generously described it as a "landmark in Australian Literature" in a speech in Legislative assembly of the Northern Territory. Maurice's first official duty after being elected was to open the new school building at Wurdeja the year before and he was happy to remain connected with the community.

The first edition of the book sold out and poor Tammy was unavailable, except from libraries, for a few years and, as they had stopped publishing fiction, the Aboriginal Studies Press had no interest in printing any more copies.

The demand was still there though, and even now I receive enquiries from schools asking if I could get copies for them or, even better, inviting me to run workshops for their students. I therefore published the second edition myself and Tammy lives again in the twenty first century!

12
ARNHEM LAND

I knew nothing about the history of Arnhem Land when I arrived. In the 1970s the teaching of history in my school focused on British and European history with a bit about the colonization of New Holland. We learned about Captain Cook and Governor Philip but I could list the six wives of Henry the Eighth more eloquently than discuss the achievements of the pioneers of my own country.

In geography lessons Arnhem Land was a large blank area on our school maps. As a part of remote Australia it probably still is and few people know anything about it, but to get an understanding of why it is what it is today it's necessary to know a little about its history and its people.

Arnhem Land covers all the land east of the East Alligator River and north of the Wilton and Roper Rivers. That's about 80,000 square kilometers of coastal floodplains, near impenetrable sandstone escarpment country known as the 'Stone Country', endless forests of stringybark, woollybutt and iron-

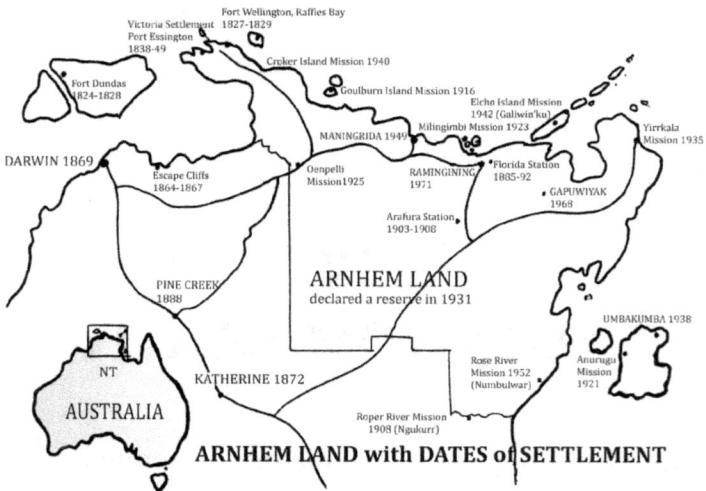

Arnhem Land map showing years of European settlement.

bark trees, mangrove swamps, flood plains and wetlands. It's an area which is home to a dozen or more Aboriginal tribes, as it has been for millennia. Tribal areas in Arnhem Land were never large like those found in the desert regions. The country here is comparatively very rich with food and natural resources so people never had to go far for a meal and boundaries between tribal lands were known by everyone. These boundaries are now neatly mapped and the traditional owners' title to their lands is inalienable, but it wasn't always so.

The first English explorers to visit the coast of Central Arnhem Land went to survey parts that Matthew Flinders had missed. In 1822 Phillip Parker King was sent to search for a river 'likely to lead to an interior navigation into this great continent'. He thereafter named and mapped the navigable parts of the Liverpool River and most of the headlands and bays in the area. He left the Blyth River to be named in 1867 by Captain Francis Cadell, who specialized in river exploration. The Cadell River, a tributary to the Blyth, is named after him perhaps by himself, because the surveyor David Lindsay was already referring to it by that name 15 years later. Cadell named the Goyder River and the Tomkinson River, a tributary of the Liverpool, and others whilst he was searching for a suitable site for a northern capital. He eventually decided on land further to the west and Port Darwin was settled at last in 1869 by 135 men and women.

Europeans were late arrivals, but they left their mark as indelibly as the famous rock art in the shelters found in the sandstone cliffs scattered across the Top End. They brought guns they weren't afraid of using, diseases such as influenza, animals like rats, pigs, buffalos and cats, and weeds like *Mimosa pigra* and gambar grass. Sailors left goats on remote islands to breed and provide fresh meat for the next time they passed. More recently they introduced refined sugar, tobacco, alcohol and kava, antibiotics and family planning, basketball and rap music.

Some invaders were introduced to the area via an 1827 settlement attempt at Raffles Bay, named Fort Wellington, abandoned in 1829, and through another attempt at Port Essington, called Victoria Settlement in 1838. This was where Prussian explorer Ludwig Leichhardt arrived by foot in 1845 after a 14 month, 4,800 kilometer journey from Moreton Bay in Queensland.

Within a few more years it was clear Victoria Settlement had also failed miserably. After each attempt the settlers set their buffaloes, Timor ponies and banteng cattle free to turn feral. At Victoria the final task was to destroy their settlement so it could not be used by the Portuguese, Dutch or French and they turned their ship's cannons on their fort to raze it to the ground. Only then, I imagine with great relief, did they sail away in 1849 never to return. These days nothing is left there except a row of dilapidated chimney stacks standing mute in the forest.

Abandonment was the chance for the buffaloes. The nucleus of their herds, which had come from Raffles Bay in 1827, were the remains of the stock brought into the first European settlement in Australia north of Port Macquarie. This was Fort Dundas on Melville Island, near present day Pirlangimpi. The buffaloes were brought to Fort Dundas from Indonesia by a wallowing brig named *The Lady Nelson* in 1824. Fort Dundas was the first doomed settlement. Originally meant to be another Singapore the lonely outpost remained lonely -no one ever visited for trade or commerce and even *The Lady Nelson* was lost, its crew killed and eaten in the Banda Islands whilst on a foraging run for supplies.

Once released, the buffalo population soon numbered in the tens of thousands. They grew wild and dangerous and nothing like the docile beasts you still see these days plowing rice paddies in rural Asia. Their environmental impact was considerable and whole ecosystems were altered as they wallowed in mud holes and beat the flood plain vegetation back so there was more open water, and they made trails that allowed salt water to intrude into areas where it had never been.

After Port Essington's failure, Europeans did little on the land for many years. Francis Cadell visited by boat during his exploration of the rivers in 1867. Then, in 1883, David Lindsay, a Government surveyor and the same bloke who started off the town of Alice Springs by his discovery of 'rubies' (although they were actually garnets), led a five month overland expedition of exploration. He rode out of Katherine in a remarkable journey that took him and five others with their 23 horses east to the Roper River, north to Blue Mud Bay and west over to Castlereagh Bay. He encountered local tribesmen aplenty when he was attacked on the Goyder River by about 300 warriors and he was harassed continually. Some of his horses were speared and local people set fire to the country around him. He may not have felt welcome, but he was thick skinned enough to return in a second survey to eastern Arnhem Land in 1917, albeit after 37 years.

Despite his warnings of the troubles with the 'blacks', Lindsay's report on the country inspired the 1885 establishment of Florida Station, an 8,000 square kilometer spread near the Glyde Inlet in Castlereagh Bay east of Milingimbi Island. Lindsay described the country as "really magnificent, either for grazing or agriculture, and unsurpassed in the Northern Territory, these magnificent plains extend for 40 miles."

Florida Station was leased by a Mr J A Macartney who had his manager, Mr Randall, drive a mob of cattle in from Waverley Station. They employed Chinese 'coolie' labour to build a cypress pine homestead on the beautiful Horseshoe Billabong. There was an English stockman named Epworth, and a French cook named Louis Fayre, whose specialty was *bouillabaisse de barramundi*! One man in the 'coolie' labour gang wasn't Chinese at all. He was Charley Araby, an African and an ex-slave who died in Darwin in the 1950s as one of the Territory's great characters.

Everything started off well at Florida. A quixotic journalist, who visited soon after the station was established wrote for the *South Australian Register* and waxed lyrical about the beauty of the country. He said that Florida Station "might without exaggeration be styled as *'A Squatter's Paradise'*," and that there was, "nothing finer than Florida."

He had some forewarning as to what was to come, it seems, as he also wrote:

> "The pioneers of Arnhem Land may at first experience some little trouble with the natives, but that will be easily overcome. A few well applied judicious lessons may be necessary, after which I think it will be found that the natives will prove of considerable value in working the stations."

He didn't linger on what a *judicious lesson* might be but one of them was a cart load of poisoned horse meat which was presented to the tribe. It was heartily tucked into by men, woman and children alike, killing many.

So, beautiful though the country may be, the settlers were quickly at war with the land owners.

The local tribesmen clearly saw Randall and his staff as invaders of their land and, of course, they speared cattle for food or perhaps out of spite. Two Malay workers, Ali and Salim, were speared in 1888. Their bodies were never found but their clothing was discovered spread around a campsite. Punitive expeditions with elephant guns, the famous Martini-Henry rifles, followed. The white men in their cypress pine, tin roofed homestead lived in such fear that they slept every night with their *nine inch colts.*

E O Robinson, who ran a supply boat out from Darwin about every six months, reported he would never approach the homestead without firing a shot first and waiting for a shot in reply. He said he always expected the men would be dead or insane by the time he returned to the station.

In 1892 Macartney gave up and dismantled his house and sent anything valuable back to Darwin on the steamer *Adelaide* Jack Watson and a party of stockmen were employed to round up what was left of his cattle and quit Florida. They drove them west to Auvergne Station, near the Western Australian border, and never returned. Jack Watson was the son a George Watson who was for many years the starter of the Melbourne Cup. He was a wild and reckless fellow apparently who would, "charge hell with a bucket of water." He was also, according to contemporary accounts, a merciless slayer of Aborigines. He was known to have, "the blacks of Blue Mud and Caledon Bays good hombres, but he had to wipe out a lot to make them so." Watson, "threw the lead at them, and threw it to kill."

The next Europeans came in 1903. Arafura Station was leased and established south of where Ramingining is now by 'Cap 'n Joe' Bradshaw, at enormous expense. One of his major investors was Sir John Cockburn, the minister for the Northern Territory in 1886 and Premier of South Australia from 1889. Already hardened to the problem of Indigenous resistance to the pastoralists Cockburn had previously ignored several outrageous massacres of Aborigines on his watch. The investors wanted the wetlands that were described as, "perfection for sugar and rice, and enough of the first rate cattle country that you'd need weeks to ride across it on a strong horse. Much of the country south and east of Ramingining became Arafura Station – it took up about 30,000 square kilometers.

It was so large it was unwieldy and the 20,000 head of cattle they brought in were naturally and easily hunted by Yolngu hunting parties. Stories indicate the cattlemen never developed good relations with the locals. Arafura Station, and hence the Premier by association, was reported by the *Northern Territory Times and Gazette* as having employed two gangs of men to shoot Aborigines on sight. In return, a mob of up to 30 locals raided a Chinese camp where they were planting cotton and killed them with Malay knives, stealing their tools and stores. At one point 70 locals rushed the station and killed, "three station natives and a half-caste". Perhaps they had reason: there's an oral history in Milingimbi of white men visiting the island from Arafura on horseback, riding around shooting children out of the trees where they'd fled to hide. Sadly it is probably true, and it's hard now to imagine how anybody could behave in this way.

Arafura Station was another abject failure and in 1908 it was also abandoned and left to the plagues of mosquitoes that still inhabit the ruins. When Cap'n Joe turned away from Arafura for the last time he left the bodies of half his Chinese and Malay workforce behind, an unknown number of Aboriginal men, women and children and more than half of the 20,000 cattle he had brought in. He was probably an embittered, wiser, but significantly poorer man.

The establishment of both Florida and Arafura stations were true invasions of a populated land, with disastrous consequences for the local tribes, but they were only two of 14 giant pastoral invasions which became 'stations' across the Territory in the late 1800s. Evidence can be easily found that, in all except two of these properties there were numerous atrocities handed out to the local people. There were more than 50 massacres in pastoral stations before 1910 and conservative estimates put the numbers killed at 600 Aborigines and 20 Europeans. The actual total will never be known. The pastoralists, backed by men in high positions, waged a war against the indigenous inhabitants of the lands they procured with Government and police support. No one was ever brought to trial for any of the crimes of this war and it was so 'forgotten' that some of the worst protagonists still have streets named after them in Darwin and Alice Springs as revered pioneers.

Despite the failure of the cattle stations there was still a fortune to be made in Arnhem Land in the hides of the feral buffaloes that now roamed with impunity throughout the wetlands. The buffalo hunting industry grew from nothing to a major industry in the early 1900s. People like Paddy Cahill, who operated in the Oenpelli region of Western Arnhem Land from 1906, are still household names. Hunters like Cahill brought tobacco sticks and metal tools as currency to employ the local men and trained them to skin buffaloes and cure their hides.

Buffalo shooting was a cruel and bloody occupation. A hunting party would shoot as many buffaloes as they could in a short time but in the hot tropics, when there is a limited window of opportunity for skinning a dead beast before it starts to decay, killing them immediately was a poor option. It was better to gallop along beside a fleeing buffalo and shoot them point blank in the lower spine to cripple them so they'd collapse to the ground and leave them to wait unable to move, sometimes for days in the heat and the flies. At last and at their leisure, the skinners would arrive to finish them off.

Also about this time missionaries began eyeing the souls to be saved. They had the best of intentions, of course. The tribes were being plagued by newly arrived diseases such as influenza, leprosy, syphilis and others, and being preyed upon by unscrupulous Europeans for their labour and sexual favours. Missionaries worked ceaselessly and fearlessly to overcome some of these problems, to the gratitude of the Government, which at that time had no systemic will, nor the ability to work on these problems itself.

At a meeting in some distant city the churches had agreed to divide the Territory up – limiting the inhabitants to the proselytizing of only one type of missionary, rather than them all. Catholics took the western Top End including Port Keats and Bathurst Island. The other churches claimed patches of Arnhem Land. The Methodists started missions at Goulburn Island, Croker Island, Milingimbi Island, and Elcho Island. The choice of islands kept the Methodists to their purpose as Methodist *Overseas* Missionaries, despite better settlement sites on the mainland. They may have been a little wary of setting up on the mainland so soon after the tragedies at Arafura and Florida Stations. Anyway, by 1935 they no longer needed to be 'overseas' in fact as well as name and they started Yirrkala Mission firmly on the mainland on Gove Peninsula. The Anglicans were awarded free reign at Oenpelli, Roper River and Groote Eylandt in the form of the Church Missionary Society. In 1920 the first Aboriginal Reserve was established at Oenpelli (Kunbarlanya). One of the reasons given was an attempt to control the contact between the Gagadju (Kakadu) and Western Kunwinjku tribes of these parts with the European buffalo shooters, where sticks of tobacco had suddenly come to be the major currency and, perhaps connected to that, light skinned babies started being born.

Light skinned babies so worried the Government and the churches that the whole sordid history of the 'Stolen Generation' was created, where babies and children as old as 16 could be taken from their mothers and brought up by strangers on missions, "for their own good." This extraordinary policy went on for more than 60 years. Jamesy Wauchope, my neighbour and a ranger in Kakadu National Park in 1983, told me the first time he'd seen white men was when he was about nine years old. In the middle of the night a number of land rovers had circled his family's camp and had left with all the mixed race children they could find and delivered them to the Mission home on Croker Island. Terrified, Jamesy, who is not mixed race, watched helplessly as his brother was taken away.

Hilda, a woman I knew who worked as a cook at Utopia School in the desert, had her children taken from her. She was in her seventies when she met up with her daughter, whom she hadn't seen for 50 years. Their reunion was filmed by the television crew who had helped her track her daughter down, and it's a film that's impossible to watch with dry eyes. Hilda had a son too, but she never managed to find him again. The Stolen Generation stories are legion and not mine to tell, but they are heartbreaking.

The Missions were established for decades before attention turned to the Liverpool and Blyth River region and by that time the necessary religious zeal to turn *every* settlement into a mission had waned and the Government's Native Affairs Branch, with its 'Aboriginal Protection Officers' took a greater role. Only a handful of Europeans had visited the region before 1955. David Lindsay passed through in 1883, and Donald Thompson, an anthropologist from Melbourne University had come close when he visited the upper reaches of the Blyth River and Cape Stewart in 1936, meeting many Burarra people and photographing several ceremonies with his glass plate cameras. Patrol Officer Gordon Sweeney walked the country around the Liverpool and Tomkinson River in 1939 and Ted Evans, a cadet patrol officer of the Native Affairs Branch, visited in 1946. Patrol Officer Syd Kyle-Little and his cadet, Jack Doolan, came in 1949 and he returned with Constable John Gordon in 1950 looking for a murderer. Photographer Axel Poignant camped on the western side of the Liverpool River and photographed ceremonies of the Kunwinjku tribe in 1952 and Ted Evans, now a patrol officer, came back with Ted Egan in 1955 to sort out trespass problems by foreign vessels in the Liverpool River. They arrested three boats and towed them back to Darwin for their Okinawan captains, who were technically Americans in those days, to stand trial.

Gordon Sweeney was an indomitable man based at the Methodist Mission on Goulburn Island in 1939. He made a two month patrol starting at the mouth of the Liverpool River where Maningrida now stands and toured Junction Bay, the Tomkinson River area and the upper reaches of the Liverpool. It was on this trip that he found a source of fresh water and thus identified the site that would become Maningrida. The aim of his patrol was firstly to visit as many of the people of the region as he could find. He achieved this exceptionally well and was warmly met wherever he went. He was invited to watch ceremonies like bone pole funeral 'corroborees' and this led to a number of semi-permanent dry season camps to meet with people. Some people followed him from camp to camp and set up their camps beside his. He was able to survey a wide variety of people for their health status, to discover how extant the traditional practices of the groups were, find out which groups circumcised their boys and which groups did not, and also map tribal and language boundaries. He made judgements about the health of languages, who spoke them, and which ones were headed for extinction and he identified the *lingua franca* of the region at the time to be Kunwinjku. Sweeney also recorded groups whose numbers were dwindling because many of the young people had headed west to the buffalo and railway camps, some as far away as Katherine and Pine Creek. The further west he travelled the more the people were inclined to immigrate towards the bright lights of the Balanda camps where tobacco, sugar and flour might be available.

The other reasons for Sweeney's patrol were either economic or functional. He discovered where the viable stands of cypress pines were for a future timber industry, the best possible agricultural areas and sites for establishing stations or homesteads, and where the major sources of food for the local people could be found. He was particularly interested in a plant he called *rakai*, which is a Milingimbi word for what the Kunwinjku called *manggulmij* or *golaj*. It is *Cyperus* sedge that grows on flood plains with a nut-like root and it is the staple diet of wild fowl like magpie geese and burdekin ducks, as well as the local people. Dry season camps could often be found on the edge of these flood plains so people could access the nuts (and the geese) easily. Sweeney also, incidentally, discovered two trees of historical importance – one blazed by David Lindsay in 1883, and another by Leichardt in 1846.

In later years Gordon Sweeney was the boss at the Native Affairs Branch in Darwin. He was instrumental in the establishment of Maningrida, although that actually happened a year after he retired, but in 1939 he was clearly a missionary first and foremost. During his patrol he held services with his patrol team of carriers, boat operators etc, in front of the local tribes, showing them photographs of other Aborigines worshipping at the missions. His report ends with advice for missionaries to undertake annual dry season patrols to the area so that:

> "The missionary could identify himself to a much greater extent with the life of the people and demonstrate his real interest in their life on their own hunting grounds… All the opportunities for service .. by a mind intent on the kingdom of God, to the work of the Kingdom in which these people have their places. And many opportunities would come for sharing with them the Good News of God's love and purposes, and for passing on the Word given us to speak."

But World War Two interrupted any possible annual return by missionaries, and people were left to their own devices for another few seasons. Ted Evans was the first to make a patrol after the war, in 1946. He and Constable Henry Lullfitz rode out of Maranboy in southern Arnhem Land after complaints that some Rembarrnga people were damming rivers and cattle were dying of thirst at Mainoru Station. Their patrol took them into the area just south of

Maningrida and Ramingining but they had little contact with people.

In 1949 Syd Kyle-Little was the first Balanda to cross Arnhem Land from north to south and the first to visit the people in the Liverpool River area in the twentieth century as a 'Protector of Aborigines'. In his two journeys he went by foot on patrol firstly right up the Liverpool River into the Stone Country past Havelock and Cuthbertson Falls and then the next year, with Constable Gordon, right across the Stone Country to the southern side of Arnhem Land and Mainoru Station, east of Katherine. In his book, *Whispering Wind: Adventures in Arnhem Land*, Kyle-Little describes his encounters with the Kunwinjku and Rembarrnga people on this river, particularly an old medicine man named Mahrdei who distrusted Kyle-Little intensely during their first encounters.

Mahrdei was the senior man and tribal leader at a 'crocodile corroboree' held on a billabong a few hundred meters from where the Mumeka community is now. Hundreds of people had been in ceremony and feeding crocodiles for days and many large crocs had gathered. Mahrdei had painted himself up as a skeleton and had danced whilst the tribe sang. Kyle-Little had watched all this as if hypnotized and had done nothing as the old man had entered the water among the crocodiles and disappeared under the murky surface. He wrote:

> "I was suddenly acutely conscious of the horror of this spot, the rank, awful smell of decaying animals, the hot

malodour of the crocodile droppings. It was an unclean place, a fitting hell hole for the evil old man's death."

But of course Mahrdei had burst out of the water a minute later, triumphant in his survival among the well fed crocodiles and his power and reputation as a medicine man was sealed.

"Him properly number one medicine man, Boss," was the comment of his employee, Oondabund.

Forty years later I saw no ceremony like this but there were times of secret 'business' often, to which I was never invited, and I couldn't write of it even if I had been. I had to be content to read the stories of the first white men to the area and talk with the elders who remembered the times. I was teaching the grandchildren of these elders, and they now lived in an era so different to their childhood that it was almost unfathomable.

Oondabund, known when I was there as Jocky Bundabunda, and another old man named Johnny Narlebar, were Kyle-Little's 'boys' throughout his patrols in 1949. When I lived in Maningrida they were still alive and lived in the community as venerable old men. Jocky was a large man with snow white hair. He lived in a house under the grand daddy of all African mahogany trees with a trunk it would take four men to reach around. In his later years Jocky would spend most of his time sitting in the shade of this tree watching his grandchildren play in the sand.

Johnny Narlebar was the opposite. A little old man as thin as a rake, he was anywhere and everywhere. It seemed he was never still and I'd see him pass several times a day wherever I was in Maningrida. He wore a blue baseball cap and was always ready with a cheery greeting.

Kyle-Little came back to Maningrida in 1993 to visit his old friends. By then well into his eighties, he was another big man and, for his age mightily strong which, I guess, is what you'd expect from a pioneer, war hero and intrepid explorer. What changes these three men had seen!

When Kyle-Little and cadet patrol officer Jack Doolan started a trading post at Maningrida in 1949, they had figured that if they could provide the western goods that were fast becoming necessities of life, through trading with the Arnhem Landers, they would stay on their tribal lands and could maintain their culture and develop their economy at the same time. The site was chosen by Gordon Sweeney because it had fresh water, but also because it was equidistant between Goulburn Island and Milingimbi Missions, and so not within anyone's pious sphere of influence.

Some of the people living in the Liverpool and Blyth Rivers area were 'traditional' and may have deliberately, or through isolation or fear, avoided contact with Europeans. Others, especially young men, sometimes travelled to the missions, or worked with buffalo hunters as skinners for a payment of stick tobacco. For decades the local tribes must have heard stories of the killings a few days walk east and of the buffalo hunters in the west and of the missionaries on the islands. They would have all gossiped about the strange men from foreign lands with technologies that were as foreign as if they'd come from Mars, and many must have been extremely curious.

The outside world was becoming curious also. Axel Poignant's 1952 photographic expedition to the western banks of the mouth of the Liverpool River left us a record in thousands of photographs of the times. His incredible images document camp life and a *Rom* ceremony offering a rare insight into how people lived in those days. Many of his photographs were published in the book *Encounter at Nagalarramba*.

World War Two brought many changes to the hopes and aspirations of Arnhem Landers. By 1947 many people had started to move away from the bush to be close to the source of western goods and services and although few Balanda made it into the Liverpool and Blyth Rivers region, large numbers of people had journeyed out. An official head count in Darwin in 1955 found 25 Aborigines from the Liverpool River and 90 from the Blyth River region living in Darwin.

At a loss about what to do, the Native Affairs Department rounded up unemployed Arnhem Landers and shipped them back to the bush several times. On the face of it this seems paternalistic at best or racist, but it wasn't necessarily a bad thing as people were often ready and willing to go. They would get free transport, and a chance to visit with their relatives, attend important ceremonies and catch up with friends. Then they'd walk back the 320 kilometers to the bright lights of Darwin. Even today young men living in the remotest outstation save up their money for months for their city holiday, though they choose to fly to the city rather than walk.

From their bark-walled trading post Kyle-Little and Doolan taught the local men how to skin and prepare crocodile skins for sale, encouraged and bought weavings from the women, attended the sick and generally tried to raise the economic standard of life for a people whose traditional culture seemed to be collapsing around them. They showed tremendous bushmanship and a humanity towards the locals that is heart-warming. Unfortunately their endeavours were for naught when the powers that be in the Government changed their minds and cancelled their program the next year. Both men resigned in disgust and their careers took different paths.

Kyle-Little had reported that leprosy was taking a toll among the Arnhem Landers and there was some pressure on the Government to do something about it. There was also the continuing problem of the drift to Darwin by people who had nowhere to live, nowhere to go and nothing to do when they got there. It took till 1957 before a serious attempt to start a community in the region actually happened. The founders were Dave and Ingrid Drysdale who had missionary backgrounds, and Trevor Millikin and Ted Egan, the Government patrol officers.

The remarkable Ingrid Drysdale was certainly the first white women in the Maningrida area and she wrote a lively account of her experiences in her memoirs *The End of Dreaming*. She was an amazing woman who had a magnificently positive effect on the men and women who visited the early settlement.

For four years she cared for any lepers brought in by families or the patrol officers and she nursed the injured. Leprosy was a fairly recent introduction to Arnhem Land, brought in by foreigners, but for the first time people had access to modern medicines, and there is no doubt they made a big difference to many people. The Maningrida leprosarium was known as Alamaise, but when the general hospital was built a few years later it was called the Ingrid Drysdale Hospital to commemorate her work in Maningrida.

Trevor Millikin also lived in Maningrida for a number of its first years and would patrol out into the bush on foot looking for people in need, like the sick and elderly, and gently encourage them to come to the settlement.

Most in the Northern Territory know Ted Egan through his music at folk clubs and as a raconteur, bush balladeer and poet, song writer and as the entertainer who invented the 'lager phone' (a rhythm instrument he plays by tapping fingers on an empty beer carton). Or, as *The Honourable* Ted Egan, Officer of the Order of Australia, the eighteenth Administrator of the Northern Territory from 2003 till 2007. He is no doubt the only Queen's representative ever to play a beer carton and sing songs to the guests at official Government events.

When I asked the old men at Gamardi and Wurdeja if they remembered Ted's first patrols around the Blyth River in 1955 they were enthusiastic in their replies. Of course they remembered and they spoke fondly of him. As one of the first white men on the Anamaiyera Plains and at Koepanga on the Blyth River, and walking through to Milingimbi, he would have been hard to forget. He's remembered in communities across the Northern Territory in other ways too. On my travels around the Territory I met a number of old men named Ted Egan because in the 1960s it was common for Aboriginal people to take on Balanda names for the Government census, and Ted's name was as good as any. Other famous names were taken too – there was a Kris Kristopherson at Canon Hill, a Robert Redford at Buluhkaduru, and Tommy Steele at Wurdeja, for example.

Before 1957 the only other non-Aboriginal visitors to come to this area had been coming for a long time. All along the north coast the ocean-going Maccassan *prahus* from Indonesia had been visiting and collecting sea cucumbers (*Bêche de Mer*) for more than 300 years. They stopped coming to the Arnhem Land coast in 1906 when the Australian Government revoked their permits, but the memory is still so alive, I know men of 50 who will swear they remember Maccassans visiting when they were young.

Japanese pearlers and fishermen also visited the north coast before World War Two. On Melville Island they almost certainly left some of their genes as there are a number of very Japanese looking Tiwi around and there are also some Japanese graves in the north of the island. One old man from Pirlangimpi told me that when he and his mates were kids they used to watch as Japanese sailors would come ashore and leave offerings on the graves for their ancestors. The kids would wait until they'd gone, then go and eat the rice cakes and other treats they left. Everyone was a winner.

Japanese pearlers are also rumoured to have planted a bed of pearl oysters off Cape Stuart not far from Yilan. Syd Kyle-Little tried to find it, unsuccessfully, but who knows - it might still be out there.

Some of the Arnhem Landers were adventurous and many were employed by the Maccassans or Japanese and a few people actually travelled with them in their boats. Even some of the Kunwinjku tribe, who were not coastal people, may have spent time with the Japanese. One old man who, it is said, had 23 wives when he died in the 1970s, could speak fluent Japanese. He claimed he'd spent time as a young man working on a pearling lugger and had lived for an off season or two in Japan.

During World War Two there was an American Air Force base on Milingimbi and there's a wrecked plane just outside the school yard there even today. Plane movements would have been regular and the tribes around the Maningrida area would have seen planes coming and going often. They would have known something was afoot and some would have journeyed to Milingimbi to see what was happening. The war was a harbinger of great and very fast change to the people of the Blyth and Liverpool Rivers region.

Darwin was bombed by the Japanese Air Force in February 1942. Soon after, some Burarra people of Cape Stewart, 30 kilometers west of Milingimbi, experienced their own little piece of the war.

Wamutjan was a young girl who was hunting crabs with her family at low tide. Along that coast the tide goes out and leaves kilometers of empty sand flats and nowhere to hide if you're walking along it. Crabs can easily be pulled out of their holes in the sand and the family had been successful. Full dilly bags of mud crabs were slung over their shoulders ready for taking home, the claws wisely broken off the still living bodies to avoid painful bites.

Wamutjan heard the noise of a plane and squinted against the brightness of the sky to spot it before her sisters.

"There, *Mununa*," she called excitedly to her grandmother.

The family saw a lone fighter plane flying low over the beach. The pilot had clearly seen them too, as he altered his direction slightly to fly directly over the little group. The kids waved in excitement, they had seen many planes heading to Milingimbi before.

But suddenly flashes of light could be seen coming from the guns under the plane. Without warning the little group was strafed with machine gun fire. I never heard how many were killed but at least one survived. Wamutjan, a little old lady in 1992, died after living for 50 years with her legs badly scarred from several machine gun bullets fired at her family that day.

No one knows if the plane was Japanese or American.

13
GROWING PAINS OF A BUSH TOWN

The Kunavidji land owners of the Maningrida side of the Liverpool River were initially very welcoming, and in fact were major contributors to the establishment of the community. Ted Egan told me that the Kunavidji had in fact asked for the establishment of a community there. Jocky Bunda-Bunda, a major land owner of the site, had been picked up by the *Tamora* as the founding party sailed past Goulburn Island. Johnny Naliba was living in the bush nearby, so he appeared early on too. They called the place *Mane Djang Karirra,* which means the 'place where the Dreaming changed shape', or more simply *Manayingkarirra,* which is pretty hard for Balanda to say, so it quickly became Maningrida.

When the Drysdales, Millikin and Egan arrived in 1957 the bush was fairly undisturbed. Ted Egan says there was almost no sign of people having lived there at all, although Kyle-Little and Doolan's well, down by the foreshore, had been walled with timber, but by whom it's hard to say as Japanese pearlers were often off the coast and they too needed reliable sources of water. Kyle-Little's bark trading post had long been eaten out by the ubiquitous termites or burned in dry season fires.

Gordon Sweeney had done his homework well. He had walked most of the country and knew that the small billabong at Maningrida was the most, if not the only, reliable fresh water source along that section of the coast. Sweeney was an ex-missionary and a surveyor, and a fearless yet humourless man known for straight talk both in English and several Aboriginal languages of Arnhem Land. The school at Maningrida was originally called the Gordon Sweeney School, but by the time I arrived his name was disappearing from the collective memory. I worked at the less personally named Maningrida Community Education Centre.

Maningrida was a success in the first few years when its population stabilized for a time at about 40 people. It was never meant to become a residential community but more a service centre for trade goods and a welfare centre for the sick. After a time it grew faster. Mrs Drysdale established a leprosarium and lepers would be brought in by the patrol officers or the families of the afflicted.

Leprosy was a disease that had been around during the days of Florida Station 60 years before. C E Gaunt wrote at the time:

> "The Macassar men, Malays and Japs trepanging on the coast for ages had left a terrible legacy to the Aboriginal.

There is no doubt that this disease or the seed had been sown among the blacks for ages, handed down from fathers to children."

Gaunt had seen leper camps as he was droving cattle and reported them to the police. He says that Mounted Constable M C Stott had replied that they could do nothing in the matter and that, "Lepers are not in the Police Manual, that camp is doomed anyhow," and there the matter ended. Other diseases were rife as well as this was a time when people would die of measles and other maladies we consider mild infections these days, and smallpox was still extant in the population. In fact, in 1888 there were nearly 300 suspected cases of smallpox in Darwin's quarantine hospital, nine of them dying rapidly from a "general hemorrhage beneath the skin."

Leprosy arrived in Darwin among the Chinese population in about 1882. The Darwin authorities responded by building a quarantine station on Mud Island, in the harbour, to house the Chinese lepers before their repatriation to China – but nothing was done for any Aborigines who contracted the disease. In 1930, Channel Island Leprosarium, essentially another island jail, was commissioned and all lepers, including any Aboriginal sufferers, were sent there for isolation. Records of 443 leprosy patients show that most were Aborigines and at least 142 died and were buried on the island. They were always short of water and with poor food the conditions were deplorable. In 1955 a more humane leprosarium was built at East Arm and staffed by Catholic nuns until 1982, when leprosy sufferers joined the mainstream medical health system and went to Darwin hospital.

Fear of the disease throughout the first part of the 1900s meant that lepers were rounded up by force if necessary. People would see their relatives taken, often to never return, and many were frightened – going to Darwin to hospital could mean a death sentence. So people preferred to hide in the bush, but when Mrs Drysdale began the hospice at Maningrida things changed. Families could set up camp nearby and stay whilst people were being cared for and the community started to grow and become more permanent. It was a welfare settlement in action as well as name, and people quickly became used to being cared for, with sugar, flour and tobacco becoming more and more easily attainable.

These were rapid changes for a society that had traditionally been spread out in distinct tribal areas. Maningrida became the home for people from many local tribes: Kunavidji, Nakkara, Burarra, Gunnartpa, Rembarrnga, Kunwinjku, Djinang, Kune, Dangbon, Gurrgoni, Wulaki and others. All these tribes spoke distinct languages or dialects and so Maningrida quickly became, for its size, undoubtedly the most linguistically diverse town in Australia. Darwin town planners liked some of these names and today the suburbs of Wulagi (*Wulaki*) and Nakara (*Nakkara*) share the glory of Milner, Stuart and other individuals worthy of being immortalized as suburbs of the city.

Occasionally Maningrida receives criticism because of its artificial origins but the reasons for its establishment were a function of the times. The Government was intent on stopping people moving to

Darwin, there were lepers who would refuse to go to Darwin out of fear, and there were pesky fishermen from Okinawa and visitors from Japan who wanted to take away pearls. People can therefore assume the establishment of Maningrida was racist, paternalistic or xenophobic according to their points of reference, but it is what it is, and it was established by some remarkable people who were highly respectful of the locals and working with the best of intentions.

In the sixties, as the welfare side of the community continued, attempts were made at turning the tribes into farmers or foresters. Market gardens were established at Cadell River (Gochan Jiny-Jirra) in 1968 where Bob Collins (later senator) worked as a young man. Some men became foresters. A sawmill was built at the top of the town to process the wild harvested termite-resistant cyprus pine and plantations were put in south of the town. A few kilometers south of the ruins of the sawmill there still existed a fire tower we used to climb occasionally to watch the sunset. Looking out across the endless forest, I could never really imagine people sitting there with binoculars glued to their eyes, watching for fires, radioing Maningrida and fire engines screaming off into the bush with teams of firefighters intent on extinguishing any blaze. They would have been busy – in the dry season most of the bush ends up burning every year.

Salaries for Aboriginal workers were poor. By the 1960s Aborigines were being paid wages, rather than food in lieu of money, but sometimes the employers would be charging for accommodation, food, power and water first, so little cash was handed over. The missions paid their men percentages of the Australian basic wage for men. In 1961 they were paying 19%, but by 1968 it had risen to 49%. It wasn't until 1973 that award wages were introduced in communities.

Perhaps the major problem for the town was its diversity. All these tribal groups were crowding in on Kunavidji land in a way that had never happened before in Arnhem Land's history. It was unnatural and stresses began to fester and grow with the community. By 1970 there were more than a thousand Aborigines living in the community and more than 200 Europeans. Cracks were beginning to show.

Many people were no longer hunter-gatherers but had become more and more dependent on social welfare and peculiar 'make-work' schemes run by the Government. Not everyone of course - some people only came to town intermittently, or would return to their clan lands when the seasons were amenable, and others were skilled workers, fully employed in the community, albeit earning a pittance.

Peter O'Connor, the CEO of the Maningrida settlement in 1974, said they never paid anyone the dole. People were expected to work for money:

> "Every person on our workforce worked on an hourly basis and attended for as many hours as they wished. In this way we spread our employment budget over a much larger group of people, as the average employee wished to work only 20 hours a week. Our way proved to be more desirable and rewarding than to arrange working for the dole as was applied in later years."

Dissatisfaction grew. Some people wanted to be on their own land, but needed the welfare controlled by Balanda. Eventually they were just paid the dole, as other unemployed Australians are. They called it 'sit down money', and even Prime Minister Bob Hawke was supposed to have encouraged an old man to 'sit down', "Don't worry, the Government will pay you to do nothing," he is said to have told him. So started a decade of increasing dependence and a correlated loss of work force skills.

In the late 1960s elsewhere in the Territory, Vincent Lingiari was leader of the seven year strike, the longest in Australian history, in the Gurindji walk-off from cattle stations in the west. The famous bark petition had been tabled in parliament by Mawalan Marika and other Yolngu from East Arnhem Land (initially to the mirth of the parliamentarians). The term *Land Rights* entered the vernacular and eventually Prime Minister Gough Whitlam set them in stone, symbolically pouring a handful of soil into Lingiari's hand at Wave Hill (Kalkaringi) in 1975. Some of the big picture politics around Land Rights passed Maningrida by because of the 'Aboriginal reserve' status of Arnhem Land. People were never really dispossessed of their lands in the local area and they retained ties to their traditional country because the small invasions by cattle men over the preceding hundred years had all failed, albeit with a trail of death behind them.

A number of people who became high profile members of the Northern Territory community for a time were Aborigines. For example, Silas Roberts came from Ngukurr on the Roper River in south eastern Arnhem Land. He worked as a health worker and rose to be adviser to John Hunter, the superintendent at Maningrida, and then chairman of the Northern Land Council, president of the Maningrida Progress Association and the Housing Association, and president of the North Australian Legal Aid Society. In 1974 he was appointed the first Aboriginal justice of the peace and special magistrate. I felt a very tenuous connection with Silas because I was at school in the 1970s when we studied Douglas Lockward's highly successful book *I, The Aborigine* which, essentially, was his brother Philip's life story.

From 1969 through till 1974 a small weekly magazine was typed and published by volunteers from the community. It was called *The Mirage* and more than 200 editions were faithfully released for an annual subscription of 50 cents. *The Mirage* is a window into the life and times of both the Aboriginal and Balanda living at Maningrida in those years. It was a warts-and-all expose of community feelings, as it was meant to be. Dan Gillespie, Maningrida administrator and occasional editor of it, wrote that *The Mirage* was 'a medium for expressing views of the people of Maningrida, and for keeping the people in touch with what was happening in our ever-changing community'.

Give people a chance to whinge and they'll generally take it. Amid all the gossip and information about births and deaths, fishing stories, basketball games and school news, there were letters and articles of vitriol and dispute. Some people weren't happy about the number of Balanda living in the community. With a burgeoning forestry industry, attempts at farming and commercial fishing and the leviathan Aboriginal Affairs Department's public servants, it was a large community indeed. Between two and three hundred Balanda lived in the community, including their families. Rita Djitmu, who worked at the school in the years I lived there, was a firebrand in the early seventies, and as a literate Kunavidʹi became a spokesperson for her people. In 1974 she was complaining about the increasing number of Balanda in Maningrida. She wrote 'now we have many Balanda and many are cheeky they think we are less people and dirty ones too... my people are not happy'.

She wasn't alone and there were major changes because of this type of feeling. Elizabeth Pearce, an ALP candidate claiming to be a blood relation of Silas Roberts, ran for office in the 1974 elections and stood on the platform saying that, "too many white people are damaging this country," and, "don't let the white man think for you." In August 1974 the Maningrida Council cancelled the permits of the foresters living in town, effectively throwing them out, with the intent to manage the forestry production themselves.

There were of course successful events and organizations in the community: the 1969 establishment of a scout troop (which was still talked about in the nineties); an exciting basketball competition and inter-community sports trips; the forestry operation including the sawmill was massive (although doomed to last only a few more months after the foresters were expelled in 1974, it was both milling wild cypress pine stands and putting in extensive plantations); new road works opened up the country to travellers; the decreasing occurrence of leprosy. *The Mirage* had stories about them all.

With the double stress of the high pressures of many tribes living in close quarters and a deteriorating relationship with the Balanda in the community, for many people it was clearly high time for a move to the homelands. The feelings at Maningrida were a reflection of a national sentiment and amid all the political turmoil Government policies did change. The early seventies became a time of 'decentralisation' at many communities as part of the Outstation or Homelands Movement. In 1968 Cadell Gardens at Gochan Jiny-Jirra was already a settlement because of the market gardens being run by Balanda, so it was a precursor of the outstation that it was to become. Other communities were established over the next few years and the process snowballed so that by 1978 there were 27 outstations supported by Maningrida. Dan Gillespie was at the Maningrida forefront encouraging the outstation movement and wrote in *The Mirage*:

> "This dry season would be an ideal time for the Government to establish its support role for those people trying to shake off the Maningrida machine."

Not all outstations were occupied all year round but some became the next best thing to permanent camps. The outstations I worked with were all established in the 1970s: Mumeka (Momega) 1972; Marrkolidjban (Murrgulidban) 1973; Ji-marda and Gamardi 1975; Wurdeja 1977, for example.

Ji-marda was always a large outstation – some 109 people are recorded as being resident there in 1979 whilst only 14 were at Wurdeja. When I was teaching there in 1991 I was roped in and temporarily employed as a census collector. I was given a bright yellow plastic shoulder bag and a bunch of forms and after school I'd wander around the outstation and count people, and ask questions such as what religion they were:

"Are you Catholic, Protestant, Anglican, Moslem, Buddhist, or traditional Aboriginal or Torres Strait Islander Religion or none?"

"I'm traditional Aboriginal."

"But Dudley, you're an ordained minister in the Uniting Church!"

"Yeah, but I'm Aboriginal first."

On census day there were more than 100 people at Ji-marda and over 20 at Yilan. These communities had stood the test of time.

Outstations needed to be supported to remain viable and in Maningrida this meant the establishment of a new corporation, Bawinanga Aboriginal Corporation (BAC) in 1974. BAC is one of the oldest outstation resource organizations and it's now an incorporated body run by an executive committee of outstation leaders elected every year at an annual general meeting. It has always had an executive chief officer and when I arrived in 1989 the erudite David Bond had been in the position for many years. As outstation teachers we often worked closely with Bawinanga and we maintained good relationships with David Bond and the BAC team.

BAC's aims have always been community development, maintenance of traditional culture and practice, the provision of training, housing and communications and to promote business and the economic independence of its members. The Maningrida Arts and Culture Centre and Djomi Museum are a part of Bawinanga, for example, and some of Australia's best known Aboriginal artists market through them.

Bawinanga had started a mud brick factory at Maningrida in the mid 1980s and beautiful terracotta houses were being built in the outstations. Generally two or four rooms inside with a space for an outside kitchen and a veranda big enough for the whole family to sit on, these were a vast improvement on the tin walled shacks built previously because they were cool and resistant to all but the most vigorous child with a hammer. They also looked great.

From 1989 a new model of welfare was introduced into the outstations. People would have to work for their dole money in a program called Community Development and Employment Program, or CDEP. This was the time I came on the scene and I was working in several outstations when the CDEP wave washed over them. At first we found it confusing. At Buluhkaduru and Borlkdjam the bush was clear felled and beaten back and the communities became dust bowls. Men and women in new boots and blue *Hard Yakka* work clothes would walk around the communities carrying chainsaws or rakes. Zoe Morgan, the regular visiting teacher at the Rembarrnga outstation schools, and I were certain CDEP must have meant the *Clear and Destroy Everything Program*. The piles of timber heaped up at Borlkdjam by a tractor burned for weeks before they were gone and Zoe complained of sore eyes from the smoke as she taught at Borlkdjam School. Our consternation was short lived though, as planting programs of mango and other fruit trees were soon introduced - the outstations began to look like the gardens they could be and we could observe the pride community members had in their handiwork.

From the beginning outstations needed support. Apart from education, the shop and the Maningrida Health Clinic both began regular visits. The original 'bush tucker man', in the *tucker truck,* would make weekly visits from the shop taking people cheques and the food and equipment they needed to purchase in one efficient journey. Prices were always high, of course, but the service was exceptional as it allowed people to stay on their homelands in relative comfort. The bush tucker man when I was in Maningrida was Peter Toms, father of four kids at the school and husband of Karen (who was eventually the Principal of the school for a few years). In the wet season Peter and his Burarra offsider, Michael Brown from Ji-marda, started running a 'tucker boat' which could go both up the Liverpool River and along the coast to the Blyth River as far upstream as Gamardi to bring supplies. They also used aeroplanes to go inland to outstations which were cut off by water.

The Health Clinic would also make regular clinic visits and weigh babies and treat disorders. They could organize air ambulances in an emergency. The leader there for many years was the fearless Sister Helen Matthews, whose achievements in health warrant a book on their own. She told once me she had delivered more than 500 babies and still knew them all. If you were ill she would be the person to see - more than a few people would prefer to consult Helen for her medical knowledge than a fly in-fly out doctor.

Schools started to open up in the outstations soon after they were established. The Principal of Maningrida School, then called the Gordon Sweeney School, was Brian Deslandes. He published the Outstation Schools Policy in The Mirage in 1974 and it had not changed by the time I was starting schools nearly 20 years later. It said basically that it was up to the community to request and support a school, including providing a living space for a visiting teacher, suitable structures for the school, and to identify a member of their community to be a teacher in the school.

Schools came and went and a parade of visiting teachers arrived over the years, each contributing what they could. Some left reputations they may or may not have deserved, others left a legacy of literate outstation people able to fend for themselves in modern Australia.

There is the story of two lady visiting teachers in the 1980s discovered parked in the bush miles from anywhere. The tucker man saw their Land Cruiser troop carrier a little way off the road and, thinking they must have been in trouble, he investigated only to find two rather embarrassed teachers lying naked on the truck's roof, sunbathing.

Jimmy Gularawuna told a story about when he was the Ji-marda School teacher:

"There was that Balanda teacher, Don. He came out in a plane one day and he just threw some boxes of pencils out the window and flew away again. He didn't even get out. No good teacher that one, just humbug, you know."

I was a visiting teacher for four years. Who knows what stories they told about me after I left, but I was never one for sunbathing on the roof of the vehicle, and always preferred to drive rather than fly.

14
LIVING IN REMOTE AREAS

I spent 20 years living or visiting in remote parts of the Northern Territory. Some of the most isolated communities anywhere in the world are out there. Australians talk of remote places 'out past the black stump' or in the 'back of beyond'. Many communities in the NT are even further than that.

The bush is famous for attracting 'the three Ms': Missionaries, Mercenaries and Misfits. It's true enough, you see representatives of all three and some of them you even suspect of being on the run, but there are other people who go out there to learn about the locals and country and to generally have positive experiences. These are the people who leave behind a legacy of improvement. Progress in the bush is slow, but it does happen.

When I lived in remote places it never felt isolated. Indeed, our community seemed at the centre of the universe and everywhere else was remote.

Bucket-bucket – a game we invented using scoops cut from plastic bottles and two buckets. The only rule – get the ball into a bucket.

Attitude amounts to everything. In the desert I used to say Alice Springs was on the beach because the sand ran all the way to the sea.

Some people who arrive from 'down south' end up living out bush for decades. Karen Toms was one – she worked as a teacher at Maningrida so long that she raised her four children there and rose to the exulted heights of School Principal. I was at her farewell, the end of an era, when George Pascoe, an erudite Djinang man who was a qualified primary teacher and one of the leaders of the School Council, gave her a farewell speech. Working cross culturally and bilingually is a challenge, even for George.

"Here's to Karen," he said, "who arrived here so

young and beautiful so many years ago, but who is leaving old and fat, thank you…"

Not everyone is suited to life out bush, but for those that are it's a fantastic place to be. Flexibility with a sense of humour is the key, although sense of humour is a relative thing. Sometimes you don't know whether to laugh or cry:

Pat Murphy's food order didn't arrive, and after a few days he wondered where it had got to. A bit of a search turned up a carton full of rotting vegetables addressed to *Bart Morphy*. At least he had a laugh. Karl, the cantankerous old German airport manager, denied responsibility.

"Vell, how do I bloomin' know who bloomin' Bart Morvy was, ja?"

Greg, my neighbour in Maningrida, was a single bloke who ordered in two packets of pampas pastry in his food order one week. His food arrived in a much larger carton than normal and, confused, he opened it to find two giant packets of Pampers nappies. We all thought it was hilarious but Greg was mightily pissed off.

Some people are made for fun. Poor Greg one day bought a small plaster gnome and had it sitting on his front doorstep. He was very pleased with it. It was about 15 centimeters tall and was pushing a little wheelbarrow. A few weeks later Murray was in Darwin and saw a range of the gnomes for sale in K-mart and bought two more. Giggling, he and I sneaked over to Greg's house one night and exchanged his wheel barrow gnome for one with a pick and shovel. Greg didn't say anything. The next week the gnome was carrying a sack. Greg started to make enquiries.

"Who the fuck is messing with my gnome?"

When I next went to Darwin I headed straight to K-mart. There were six more different models! I bought one of each of them and for the next few months the gnomes would change every week. Greg became really annoyed by it.

"That bastard did it again, last week when you were at Gamardi!" he'd say.

He could never work out who it was and never suspected there'd be two villains at work. Murray or I were always out bush when an exchange occurred and because we used to take turns we remained above suspicion. Years later I found the original gnome in a box and tracked down Greg's address from his mother in Tasmania. I posted him his gnome, but never heard a word back from him. I guess it was one of those jokes that only Murray and I found funny. Poor Greg, if you read this please take it as an apology.

Living in the bush leads people to go to extraordinary lengths for a moment's entertainment. One bloke got up well before dawn and set up his two giant speakers on either side of his neighbour's bedroom, running the wires he'd bought especially through the garden from his amplifier. Then at the crack of dawn, in beautiful stereo and at full volume he played the soundtrack of a locomotive travelling at speed. With the stereo Doppler effects, Peter, half asleep, had the impression a train was passing right through his bedroom. He said afterwards that he'd 'nearly had kittens' and had fallen out of bed, white as the sheet he was lying on.

Trevor Burke, the bloke who took me on my first successful barramundi expedition, got me a beauty one day. He and his family had looked after Turkey the dog out in Alyangula over the Christmas holidays, and I had a transfer to a new job in Katherine in January. I arranged for Trevor to put Turkey on the plane to fly him to meet me in Darwin. The plane was late and I had to hang around for a couple of hours but at last Turkey's crate arrived and I went to pick him up. Bloody Trevor had dyed him a bright pink - his woolly locks were the shade of Barbie's packaging!

Turkey didn't seem to care and there was nothing to do about it anyway as I needed to drive to Katherine right away, so we set off. First stop was a petrol station just out of town. I was pleased that I was the only one there and I pumped the petrol with Turkey sitting bolt upright in the front seat, glowing radioactively. And then - and what are the odds of this? - the local Hell's Angels Motorcycle Club rolled in to refuel! Twenty big hairy bikers parked all around me and my pink poodle.

"… afternoon," I said quietly, nodding to them as if everything was right in the world.

"G'day mate," replied the biggest and hairiest of them all.

There were a few sideways glances but no one mentioned Turkey, so I paid for the fuel and sidled away. Phew! The next stop was Katherine, three hours away. I had a house to move into and Turkey was inside straight away. No one saw him! Why then, when I went to Woolworths for some supplies a little later, did a complete stranger turn up and say,

"G'day, are you the new Principal for Kath South?"

"Yes," I replied. "How's it going?"

"You're the one with a pink dog then?"

Great start in a new job in a new town! Bloody Trevor Burke! Revenge is a dish best served cold Trevor. I await my opportunity!

Sometimes living in the bush can mean you miss out a little on what is *normal* education in the cities. I guess this is how country bumpkins are made. In the mid 1990s someone told me the Coles Myer Company was offering shareholders with a minimum of 500 shares a seven and a half per cent discount on all purchases. At that time all my buying was through Coles Bush Orders so it seemed wise to buy 500 shares and save money. I was in Sydney in the January holidays and found myself walking past the Sydney Stock Exchange. On an impulse I went in and up to the girl on the front counter.

"G'day," I said, tipping my Akubra, and offering my hand for her to shake. "Derek Pugh from the Northern Territory!"

"Err, hello," she said. "What can I do for you?"

"Five hundred shares in Coles Myer please."

She blinked, confused.

"I beg your pardon," she replied.

"I want to buy 500 shares in Coles Myer please, I'll pay cash."

"Um, I am sorry, Sir," she said. "We don't sell shares here."

"What do you mean? Of course you do." I persisted and pointed at the giant sign above her head. "Is this the stock exchange or not?"

"Yes, it is, but you can't *buy* shares here. You have to go to a broker."

Well, how was I supposed to know that?

------- -----------

Many communities in the bush can have a high turnover of European staff. Balandas come and go. If we were in town, Murray and I sometimes got the job of picking up new arrivals from the airport because we didn't have a class to look after. We used to guess what the new arrivals were like and how long they'd stay even before they'd walked the distance from the plane to the arrivals shed. Sometimes we were extraordinarily accurate! A woman named Ally Green arrived one Monday and we stood in the shade and watched her walk across the tarmac from the plane. It was hot and through the heat shimmer on the asphalt we could tell she was nervous, taking tentative steps away from the plane, eyes darting everywhere.

"Ten days," said Murray.

"You're being generous," I said. "Five…"

We split the difference and agreed she'd last a week. Ally Green, who from day one became known as *Wattle* Green for reasons I don't really know, hated

Maningrida on sight. Exactly seven days later she flew out again back to Darwin and caught a bus down south, calling the Superintendent at every rest stop claiming she was being followed by malevolent Aborigines from Maningrida.

A teacher arrives full of promise for new input to a community, but only lasting a week, a month or a term is a tragedy for the kids. All schools need stability and commitment from good teachers to build relationships, traditions and educational successes. This is nowhere more important than in Aboriginal communities.

The most famous failure of the recruitment process for bush schools in the 1990s was when two sisters, recruited to teach at Numbulwar School in south eastern Arnhem Land, were flown out in a chartered plane. The plane circled the community and landed. A group of people from the school had come up to greet them but the girls had been so horrified by what they had seen from the air they refused to get off the plane and had to be flown back to Darwin.

New teachers attend a two or three day induction conference to help them prepare for their lives out bush and to start to learn the intricacies of the workings of The Department. In Alice Springs one year I addressed a group of new comers:

> "Arriving at a remote community from a distant city can be confronting. New experiences, new learning, harsh climates and a strange foreign culture are challenges that need to be understood and adapted to. Then, when you start to feel comfortable with a life that you find varied and exciting, going

back home to family and friends who are still doing the same humdrum things they did when you left can also be confronting. Little will change when you're away.

Friends and family cannot know in all honesty anything about what you have been experiencing. Initially you will field inane ignorant questions over and over again from people like: Do *they* eat raw meat?, Why don't *they* speak English? This is Australia!, Isn't it dangerous living there?

Eventually they will stop asking and you will stop telling. You'll just be the bush teacher in the family and everyone will get on with their lives. If you return after a few years to your home town, it will be like you've been time travelling, and have arrived back on the same day you left."

These new teachers, as all are, were full of questions. They didn't really know what to expect. I was chairing a session at this conference with a guest speaker talking about health in the bush. She was one of those salt-of-the-earth people - a remote area nurse, worth her weight in gold. Her presentation was about diet and exercise, getting fresh food in, maintaining health, vaccinations and the like, but at one time the conversation got bogged down when people started asking about the dangers of snake bites. Teachers were asking questions over and over about snakes and anti-venom medicine. Because I was chairing, when I thought they'd gone along this line long enough I tried to bring it back to more realistic issues.

"For goodness sake," I interrupted a little exasperated. "You are *not* going to get bitten by a snake! You'll be lucky to even see one."

Then Jo Pyke, a teacher from Willowra School who was helping with the conference, bless her, put her hand up.

"Don't be so sure," she said, starting another hour of circular discussions among the recruits. "I was bitten by a brown snake in the school sports storeroom last year."

Keeping in touch with family and friends 'down south' as we used to say, because that's where most new teachers came from, is very important. Longevity of bush employment might well depend on the success of maintaining distant and important relationships. In the nineties telephones arrived in Maningrida houses for the first time and for a brief period we had the most up to date telephone exchange system in Australia. It was the time when telephone banking was starting up and we also had fax machines, so we felt very advanced. I could do things on my new phone that folks down south could only dream of with their antiquated systems. These days internet and Skype cut the tyranny of distance to the bare minimum, although nothing is better, of course, than for family members to visit.

My parents came up to visit me in Maningrida during the week we ran our 'Outstation Sports Carnival'. We used to combine all the kids from Maningrida, Ramingining and Oenpelli Outstation Schools, 21 schools in total, and hold massive events attended by 400 children or more. Dad and Mum were extremely impressed with the kids - their toughness and resilience and awareness of their environment were clear to see. Mum got much stressed watching the kids playing *bucket-bucket,* a game I invented using two buckets, a ball and dozens of scoops cut from White King bleach bottles painted in team colours. The only rule was to count the goals, there were no boundaries, and even little kids would find they could catch a ball with their scoops and throw it accurately to a team member. It was fast paced and bedlam, a hundred kids stampeding through the outstation, and Mum worried incessantly that the kids would run through the cooking fires. Luckily this never happened.

Mum's biggest annoyances were finding somewhere private to go to the toilet and the squeaking of a swing, ridden incessantly by an endless lineup of small kids. The toilet problem was solved by the provision of a two liter ice cream can and the squeaking by greasing the chain with margarine. She was so happy then that she wrote an article for *Woman's Weekly* about it.

Dad, in the meantime, took on the role of lead tea maker. He spent hours tending a central fire and had giant billies of tea on the go at all times for anyone who wanted a cup. He was about the most popular adult at the carnival.

Long distance driving is an excellent time to talk and get to know one another. Dad and I dropped kids off at one of the furthest outstations after the carnival and on the drive back to Maningrida I got him talking about his Korean War experiences, which he'd never spoken of before to me. One story sticks in my memory well:

He and his men had been moving through a battlefield after the action was over. It was freezing cold and the detritus of war was everywhere. They came across bodies half buried in mud and snow. One of the bodies was all hidden except for a frozen hand sticking out of the ground, reaching skywards. Dad explained that the tension was broken when they saw it and, as he said, "some wag had put an apple in the hand."

Teachers need to be able to spend a few years in a school to really be beneficial, both for the school and for the teacher. In some communities the first few months or the first year can be hard, but as relationships develop and more is learned it gets easier in the second and third years.

The most constant and potentially valuable influences in schools are the Aboriginal teachers whose country the school is part of. A great deal of effort has been put into training and developing them to take control of education in their own community and some have risen to the challenge admirably. Some local people have shown promise and trained to take on new roles and they have become pillars of education, role models for the young and important leaders in the economic and cultural growth of their communities. People like the late Mandawuy Yunupingu, school Principal at Yirrkala and the *Yothu Yindi Band* lead singer; *Esther* Djayhgurrnga, Principal at Gunbalanya CEC; Didemain Ubo at Ngukurr and many others were the pioneers in the new future of Aboriginal culture and community advancement in the 1990s, and all the time new people are stepping forward. These are people who really make a difference.

With time, and political will, Aboriginal people will choose to become educated in a western sense and their communities will move forward. The lucky ones will be able to retain the best of their traditional culture and ties to their country. Cultures have always been dynamic, and the strong ones are able to adapt and adjust to the influence of outsiders. Education is a key to finding out how to do this. For Aborigines it will happen on their terms and the non-Aboriginal community will need to be positive and supportive rather than interventionist.

Even with a growing number of local Aboriginal teachers being trained and employed in their local school there will always be a need for good quality Balanda teachers to offer what they can to these communities. It is a fantastic learning opportunity and can offer great professional satisfaction and career advancement. However, Indigenous communities don't need 'bleeding heart liberals' who want to 'find themselves' or sort out personal problems. They need self reliant, committed, enthusiastic and energetic realists who like people in general and who really like working with kids.

Some people reading this book will be teachers, so I want to end with a call to any who fit this description and are willing to aid the development of Indigenous communities without being paternalistic missionaries, mercenaries or misfits. If you have got a thirst for adventure, like working with children, have an interest in culture, history and a positive future - and can develop a strong rapport with your students - you may have what it takes. So give it a go.

###

Also Available

Tammy Damulkurra,(2nd edition 2013)
with the Sunshine Girls of Maningrida.

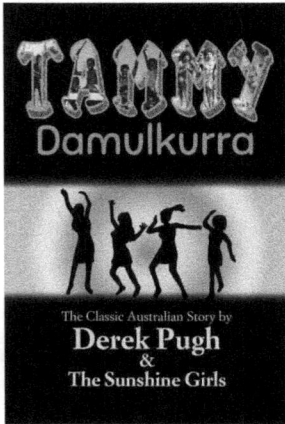

Fifteen year old Tammy Damulkurra lives in Maningrida - a remote Aboriginal community in Arnhem Land. Tammy has friends and likes the disco and thinks at last she has her first boyfriend but he cheats on her and Tammy gets into a fight with her arch enemy, Sharon. Tammy's parents send her to the outstations for several weeks to cool off and she quickly gets used to the bush and fishing and hunting with relatives. When she returns to Maningrida her love life is a mess and it's not until she leaves again for school that she realises that it's all going to be okay.

Originally released in 1995 this second edition celebrates two decades of its use in literacy education in Australian schools.

"a landmark in Australian literature" Maurice Rioli, MLA, 1995
"a story that will strike chords with many teenagers," with a "naive quality and adolescent voice (which) makes it instantly accessible" B Richardson

By Derek Pugh

The Owner's Guide to the Teenage Brain

The Owner's Guide to the Teenage Brain reveals the mysteries of modern neuroscience and teaches teenagers, parents and teachers how to prepare their brains for learning. Teenagers can maximise the efficiency of their learning and cope better with the exciting changes of the teenage years. Adults can be reminded about what is needed for optimal learning. This is powerful knowledge that gives the reader an essential edge in today's world with its high competition and crowded curriculum.

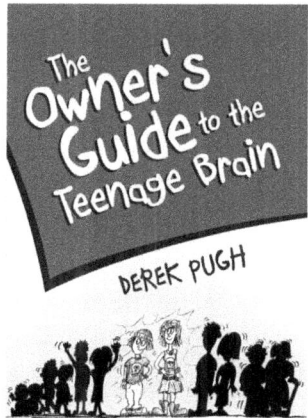

"Finally, a book written and designed about learning that will appeal to teens" Grady Harp
"Derek Pugh has got it 100% right with his new book..." Dr Mark Heyward, Education consultant

www.derekpugh.com.au

ABOUT THE AUTHOR

Derek Pugh is an author and educator with 30 years experience in schools. He has taught every level from pre-school to adults in a range of cultures in four different countries. He currently runs an international consultancy in Brain Compatible Education and he visits schools and speaks at conferences to explain how students can maximise the efficiency of their brains. He also delivers workshops on: rites of passage in modern schools; the power of story telling in education; and on literacy and creative writing based on the model he developed in writing the negotiated text novel with the 'Sunshine Girls of Maningrida' titled Tammy Damulkurra.

Derek Pugh lives with his family on the western slopes of Rinjani Volcano in Lombok, where he can look out across the Lombok Strait and watch the sun set over Bali.

He is available as a keynote speaker and presenter at conferences or schools worldwide, and can be contacted through www.derekpugh.com.au.